GIFTS

YOUR GUIDE TO CHOOSING IMAGINATIVE
AND UNUSUAL GIFTS

About the Author

Judy Hubbard has a B.A. in English from Adelaide and taught in secondary school before working as a Public Relations Consultant in Australia and abroad. Her first book *The Good Gift Book* was published in 1985.

Judy now lectures on 'Creative Gift Giving' for the Council of Adult Education in Melbourne. *Gifts* is brimming with colourful, new ideas with lots of inspiration from her students, and input from family and friends.

Married with two energetic sons, Judy also divides her time between freelance Public Relations work, home management and community activities.

Dedication   For Graham, Michael and Andrew Hubbard

Special thanks to Joy Hopper for her advice and help.

Acknowledgements: The author and publishers would like to thank the following for providing props for the photography of the book: Mid City Granny May's Paper Shop; Made Where, Double Bay; Mid City House and Garden; Lois With Love, Mosman; David Jones; Appley Hoare Antiques; Hampshire and Lowndes.

Published by Bay Books,
61–69 Anzac Parade, Kensington,
NSW 2033

Copyright Text © Judy Hubbard

National Library of Australia card number and ISBN 1 86256 268 7

Pictures from Bay Picture Library

Edited by Sheridan Carter

Designed by Edward Gillan

Illustrations by Greg Gaul

Printed in Singapore by Toppan Printing Co.

Typesetting by Savage Type Pty Ltd

BB88

GIFTS

YOUR GUIDE TO CHOOSING IMAGINATIVE
AND UNUSUAL GIFTS

JUDY HUBBARD

BAY BOOKS
Sydney and London

CONTENTS

INTRODUCTION

They say it's the thought that counts and it's certainly true that even if you spend a fortune there's no guarantee that you've picked the perfect gift.

What makes a truly *great* gift? Everyone you ask will have a different answer and, while any small gesture is likely to be warmly appreciated, coming up with a gift guaranteed to hit the spot demands a good deal more than money. So how do you devise that special something for the person who seems to have everything?

This book should provide invaluable inspiration and a wealth of ideas for novel, witty, sentimental and entertaining offerings to buy or make, plus a spectrum of goodies geared to specific lifestyles, hobbies and enthusiasms.

Giving should be just as much fun as receiving — watching a face light up as its owner opens your thoughtfully chosen and imaginatively wrapped parcel is pure pleasure — and ample reward for all the time, trouble and money spent. It also smooths the way on big social occasions and eloquently expresses hard-to-voice sentiments — a single red rose may seem the most hackneyed way of saying 'I love you', but it's never been known to fail! If you've little cash to splash around, *making* a present implies a generosity of time and spirit that is far more touching than a hastily-packaged gift lifted off a shop counter half an hour beforehand.

Lots of well-intended and costly offerings miss their mark because so many of us unconsciously give what we ourselves would most like to receive! The secret of successful gift-giving lies in forgetting your own fantasies and making an effort to analyse the interests, tastes and style of the recipient.

Personality is a reliable pointer — would-be sophisticates yearning for nothing more than some of life's little luxuries will be frankly disappointed at receiving some worthy household item, while those with a thoroughly practical bent will pale at the prospect of a charming frivolity. It's also well worthwhile considering a person's preferred colours, their taste in clothes and decor, plus their line of work and hobbies . . . and if all these clues lead you to a crocheted loo roll cover, or a yawn-inducing book on car maintenance, simply prepare to bite the bullet! At least you'll have the pleasure of witnessing their delight at finally getting the present they'd always wanted!

Money is, of course, a major consideration, especially when contemplating classic gifts for landmark occasions like weddings, anniversaries or christenings. With a little forward planning, you needn't break the bank in acquiring, say, an exquisite piece of crystal or porcelain — these items are often heavily discounted in the half-yearly sales, so it pays to stock up on a few such treasures if you can anticipate the occasions when you might give them. Similarly, you can keep your eyes peeled all year round for reasonably priced or discounted goods, quality seconds or clever imitations, and present paraphernalia like witty gift tags, wrapping paper, ribbons and cards. Fairs, stalls and sales of work are a rich source of low cost but original offerings and packaging goodies. Holidays also present an ideal opportunity for picking up exotic and unusual knick-knacks.

But while it makes sense to plan ahead and keep a cache of gifts at the ready, this becomes a false economy if they simply gather dust in a drawer because you can never quite find the right person to receive them.

Your best bet is to keep a little black book in which you can jot down any helpful hints you get from friends and relations that could be translated into gift ideas, then map out your gift-giving calendar for the coming year. Marry the two and you should have some fairly strong guidelines to govern your present purchases, but don't forget to keep tabs on all that you've gathered — you don't want to duplicate!

Coming up with the perfect gift simply needs thought, creativity and imagination — remember that it's far more effective to present a small and exquisitely witty gift than to spend the same on an ostentatious but slightly damaged or shop-soiled item.

The cardinal rule with any gift you give is to make the recipient feel spoiled and cherished, whether it's teacher getting the shiniest red apple or your beloved being showered with treasures beyond their wildest dreams.

We hope you'll find the inspiration in this book to do just that — at least you will be sure that, whatever you've given and however much you've spent, no-one will have done it better.

Y ou wouldn't turn up at an important job interview dressed in unironed and tatty clothes, so why think you can get away with presenting a gift in the crumpled paper bag in which it came?

Many of us overlook the impact of an exquisitely wrapped and beribboned package, confident that the contents will speak for themselves. Yet imaginative presentation is the final flourish of gift-giving, an extra which attractively underlines the special care and thought that has gone into your gesture.

This chapter is packed with bright ideas for both simple and

1 ALL WRAPPED UP READY TO OPEN

elaborate trimmings which will always make *your* offerings stand out and linger long in the lucky person's memory.

We give gifts to pamper and delight, so the sight of a stylishly packaged parcel provides the first frisson of anticipation of joys to come. Though cynics may say it's a waste of time to put effort into a wrapping which will be destroyed in seconds, it undoubtedly adds style and significance to even the most ordinary gift.

Wrapping, ribboning and colourful trimmings provide a marvellous opportunity to let your imagination run wild. There is a vast range of inspired commercial packaging paraphernalia which you can mix 'n' match to meet a range of moods and colour co-ordinations, but you can add even more dash to your gesture by making your own wrappings, cards and gift tags.

With a little forward planning, thought and creativity it's amazing what eye-catching and stunningly individual ensembles you can put together — a card shaped and decorated like a house for friends on the move, a parcel decorated with a sprig of holly at Christmas time, a gift within a gift like a pair of gloves that has each finger filled with a tiny treasure.

The possibilities are endless and the added bonus with beautiful wrappings is that it's more than just the gift that will delight the recipient with wit and flair!

Mid City Granny May's Paper Shop

CARDS

A home-made card can be a delightful gift in itself because it reflects you and your personal message. Professional results are easy and quick to achieve if you have a good selection of basic materials.

Materials

- large sheets of card in a range of different colours
- a selection of plain card, sheets of bond paper, old wrapping paper and cards for cutting up
- Texta pens, coloured inks, pencils, calligraphy set, gold and silver pens
- stick-ons — stars, pictures, fabric scraps, cottons, motifs, glitter, dried flowers
- Letraset
- scissors, glue, double-sided tape, ruler, set square, hole puncher, stapler

CREATIVE CARD IDEAS

✳ stick toffee, fudge and other exotic wrapped sweets onto a simple card using double-sided tape

✳ handyman card — tape a piece of sandpaper and a selection of nails, screws and washers onto a card

✳ a collage theme card (for example, reminiscent of Victorian keepsake cards, covered with scraps, cut-outs from paper doilies, glitter and bows. To make symmetrical hearts, fold paper in half, draw half a heart, then cut out)

✳ Letraset a name onto plain card

✳ house-shaped card with opening doors and windows and comments under the flaps

✳ use fabric Texta to write your birth-day message on a handerkerchief

✳ rebus card — stick pictures, numbers and letters of the alphabet onto card (see diagram)

✳ gift tag cards — make from parcel cards or white card (use a hole puncher for holes and decorate as you like e.g. sequins, braid or glitter) or cut old cards or paper down into usable mini-cards

✳ clown card

SWEETS CARD
Wrapped Sweets stuck down with double sided tape.

FOLDING CARD
To make a folding card divide a long sheet of card into equal sections; score each join lightly to make folding easy.

With the strip of card opened out draw or paint a picture on it (e.g. caterpillar, train, snake) covering the full length of card.

Fold into the card shape and tie with a bow to hold in place.

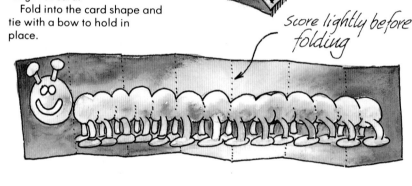

Score lightly before folding

CLOWN CARD

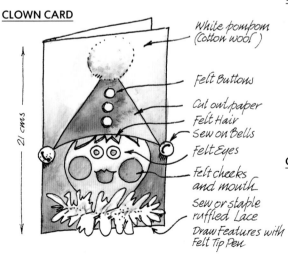

21 cms

White pompom (Cotton wool)

Felt Buttons

Cut out paper
Felt Hair
Sew on Bells
Felt Eyes

Felt cheeks and mouth

Sew or staple ruffled Lace

Draw Features with Felt Tip Pen

CARD SHAPES

Choose an appropriate shape for the card (it might be a square, a circle, a tree, a house, a teddy bear, an apple or a car). Practise drawing the shape first or make a template to use for tracing.

Cut and fold a piece of card to shape, measuring with a set square to get perfect edges if it involves straight lines. If your shape is made up of lots of contours make sure you keep one straight edge intact so the card will stand up.

If you use bond paper instead of card fold it into four layers. A4 paper folds into neat 15 cm × 10.5 cm card which stands up well.

DOTTY CARD

CUT-OUT GIFT TAG

MAKING YOUR OWN ENVELOPE

Envelopes look great in matching paper with a tiny bow, flowers or ribbon on the outside. If your wrapping paper is plain, decorate the envelope as you would a card.

ENVELOPE

Use a plain sheet of paper or patterned gift wrapping paper to make this envelope for a small card (8.5 × 13.5 cm). Add on ½ cm (.5 cm) to each measurement to create shape (5), which should measure 9 × 14 cm.

Top and side flaps need to be ½ × (4.5 cm) and bottom flap ½ × plus 2 cm to overlap (6.5 cm). Cut out flaps to correct size and shape. Fold flaps (3) and (4) into place; glue the edges of flap (1) and stick down. Fold flap (2) down, ready to glue once your card has been inserted.

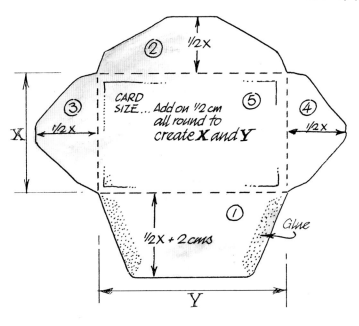

AUSTRALIANA CARD

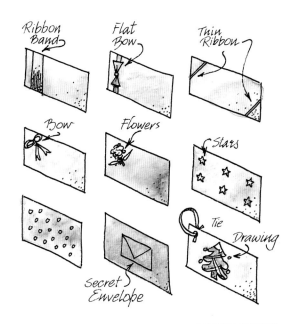

ENVELOPE TRIMMINGS

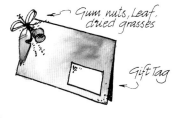

REBUS CARD

WRAPPING

Wrapping is very much the hors d'oeuvre of gift-giving. It can create a fantastic sense of anticipation and suspense; and make the act of unwrapping a real pleasure.

Materials
scissors (small and large)
stapler
clear, double-sided tape
papers (gold, silver, tissue, cellophane, doilies)
glitter, flowers, stars, transfers, felt, sequins
stickers
Letraset
glue
used boxes (e.g. shirt boxes, shoe boxes)
tulle
butterflies
shells and other tiny trinkets and baubles

SIMPLE TIPS

❋ Use boxes whenever possible (especially for a gift with a peculiar shape) as they make wrapping easier, and always look great.
❋ Scroll any odd shapes into a piece of cardboard as cylinders are easy to wrap.
❋ Use double-sided tape, or roll pieces of sticky tape for neatness and style.
❋ Be adventurous with your colour schemes e.g. black and metallic silver; black and fuchsia; pink and purple; three shades of one colour.

WRAPPING A PERFECT BOX

Box wrapping is a dying art that deserves revival. There was a time when every shopkeeper wrapped neat brown paper parcels with sharp edges and beautiful tucked ends. Here's how:

☐ Check your gift for price tags, and remove

☐ Place article upside down on paper. Always work from the bottom of your article, and put it in a box if possible.

☐ Cut the paper to size (too much paper means an untidy parcel).
To find the correct size of paper, leave a little more than half the depth of the article only on either side of the parcel. Cut away excess. Now fold paper over the top. Before cutting away, check the position of folds on the paper. Move the paper to conceal seams or edges where possible. Now cut away excess from the top.

☐ For a perfect finish, make a small hem on each end of the paper before you fold over the sides and top of the parcel. Tape down the top fold with a piece of tape at either end. Fold over the second piece, securing each end with a piece of tape near the corner.

☐ The sides! Press the paper down from the top. Make sharp corners each time. Tape at each end.

☐ Press in the sides to create a perfect point on the triangular bottom piece. Cut away paper to make this point if necessary. Secure this point underneath with rolled tape. Repeat this on the other side. Turn the parcel over and add ribbons and decorations, covering seams where possible.

WRAPPING A BOX

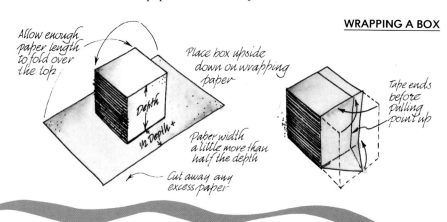

Allow enough paper length to fold over the top

Depth

½ Depth +

Cut away any excess paper

Place box upside down on wrapping paper

Paper width a little more than half the depth

Tape ends before pulling point up

PAPER GIFT BAGS

A paper gift bag makes the perfect container for a range of gifts from sweets and lipsticks to roasted nuts, and can use up all those smaller pieces of left-over gift paper. Use these instructions to make a bag of any size. These bags look particularly good made from Christmas paper, with gold ties, hung from the tree as a decoration.

☐ Make a 2 cm hem on one side of the sheet of paper.

☐ Fold a 2 cm hem at the top (this becomes the top of your bag).

☐ Roll the paper to make a cylinder, with the edges not quite meeting. Secure this side edge with double-sided tape or rolled sticky tape on the underside.

☐ Flatten the bag out, then fold 3 cm over at the bottom.

☐ Pull down one fold, and press it firmly to make points at each end.

☐ Fold down 1 cm of paper from the top flap, and a little more than 1 cm from the lower flap so that it just overlaps. Tape in place with a strip of tape.

☐ Open it out, punch holes in the top of the bag, and add ties.

PAPER GIFT BAG

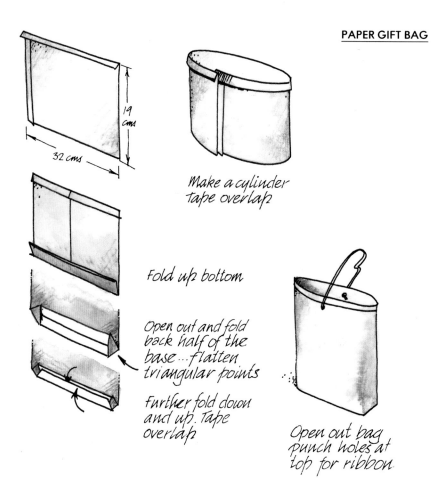

19 cms

32 cms

Make a cylinder Tape overlap

Fold up bottom

Open out and fold back half of the base...flatten triangular points

Further fold down and up. Tape overlap

Open out bag punch holes at top for ribbon

JOINING PAPER

If you are determined to giftwrap objects like an ironing board (this requires about 9 sheets of paper) you'll need to join sheets of paper together. It's useful to know how for when you have an unusual shape to wrap or not quite enough paper to go around.

Turn up a half inch hem on the first piece of paper. Lay the piece of paper to be joined on over the hem, leaving a small gap at the top. Turn over and check that the pattern matches before sticking in place. Place a piece of tape in the centre of the join. Smooth paper to the ends and tape. Add a final long strip of tape along this line. The join should be almost invisible.

Wrong Side of paper

Extra piece

Turn up hem (10mm)

Lay extra piece on hem leaving a 5mm strip of hem showing. Tape temporarily with small pieces of tape. turn paper over, check alignment of patterns turn back over and tape edge fully

PATCHWORK PAPER

Use the paper joining technique to make a sheet of original gift paper from sheets of newsprint and other papers. Make a zany design by sticking on magazine cut-outs, fabric scraps, sweet papers. Add some finishing touches with coloured crayon or felt tip pens.

PAINTED GIFT PAPER

If you like getting paint on your fingers this is for you! Make a pattern of swirls, circles, squares, basket-weave and whatever else takes your fancy on white paper using a selection of colours. This is an excellent gift project for children and making a mess is all part of the fun!

Mid City Granny May's Paper Shop

FABRIC BAGS

A simple drawstring bag makes an excellent coverup, or practical container for a gift (see p. 58).

A BUNCH OF CELLOPHANE

Gifts of hampers, boxes and baskets can look even more inviting with a flounce of cellophane. Use two sheets for bigger items, draw up to a frilly neck and tie tightly with a wide bow.

For an even more colourful finish silver or gold stars, floral stickers or tiny ribbon bows can be added.

SPECIAL OCCASION BOX

An ordinary shoe box can be decorated very stylishly for a special occasion. It can be for a purely decorative display or used as a container for small gifts.

Paint a large or small shoe box, with separate lid, using poster paint. Glue on trimmings of ribbons and bows leaving space for the central decoration (e.g. small figures; Easter eggs; Nativity scene).

For a Christmas box paint the box white or silver. Glue on wide red ribbon in a simple cross pattern and add a centre piece of pine cones, holly and a bright red fabric flower like poinsettia. This box can be used each year and may be redecorated and added to from year to year.

A GIFT WITHIN A GIFT

There are some wonderful hiding places for gifts. The gift within a gift idea adds an element of suspense and surprise to the unwrapping and can provide great amusement.

Glass kitchen jars, baskets, bags and purses, large shells, moulds, teapots, coffee mugs, jugs, flower pots, enamel tins, bucket, tea cups — these can all be loaded up with other wrapped objects, which can contain even smaller gifts!

Gifts can also be *wrapped* in other gifts: fabric (calico, cottage prints, silk, Christmas prints, lace); T-shirt; chamois; napkin, handkerchief; scarf.

RIBBONS, BOWS AND OTHER FINISHING TOUCHES

Now that your parcel is beautifully wrapped, with immaculate edges, it's time to add those special touches. It may be a simple pussy bow or something more spectacular like a three-colour fluffy bow or lattice wrap.

It's often the finishing touches like a fluffy bow, a bunch of fabric flowers or an enormous wide satin bow which add pizzazz and character to a gift.

Here are some ideas:
* stickers, dots, glitter, hearts and stars
* cut-out felt shapes
* fabric scraps and small toys (Victoriana, animals, nursery rhymes)
* jingling bells
* lettering — Letraset, a name in gold pen, or felt initials
* a single rose, a posy of tiny fabric flowers or real flowers
* paper doilies
* sweets, paper butterflies, sequins, fabric birds
* wide ribbon with thin contrast ribbon overlaid
* a string of paper hearts

HINTS

* Use contrasting colours for finishing touches like bows.
* Bows are best off centre, except on a cube parcel where the bow is centred and should cover the top completely.
* Cover folds where possible with ribbon and bows.
* Always make the tails of your bows go where you want them to go by securing with double-sided tape.

* For the square box wrap, and pussy bow, use two pieces of ribbon of different widths, placed on top of each other and glued or stapled in place.
* For bonbons, tie with two different coloured ribbons of the same length

and width, placed on top of each other. Fan the colours out after tying.
* Most ribbon can be stripped to any width. Use thinner pieces for tiny parcels, and different widths for the lattice wrap.
* When you are adding ribbon trims, test the length required before cutting. Allow ½ in for double-sided tape to overlap. Tape half to the ribbon, and half to the parcel.

BOWS WITH SPIKES

These look fabulous for special occasions. Follow the instructions for fluffy bows, till you have tied a knot in your loops.
☐ Before pulling out loops, make two cuts on each loop.
☐ Cut a thin strip starting near the first cutaway point. Do each side of the loop, but cut in the opposite direction.
☐ Cut to a point just over the top of the loop.
Note: Take special care as you pull these loops out not to tear the spikes. If you like a less spiky look, curl each spike lightly with your scissors as you would curling ribbon.

PUSSY BOWS

☐ Tie your parcel and make the knot. One end of the ribbon will naturally seem to point up and one down.
☐ Make a loop with the bottom ribbon first, then bring the top ribbon around it to make a classic bow that sits perfectly.

CHRISTMAS BOX

PUSSY CAT BOW

Take ends down

GIFT EXTRAVAGANZA

BONBON BOW

Tie using 2 colours
Fan 2nd colour out

CELLOPHANE WRAPS

SPIKY BOW

follow "Fluffy Bows" to this point
Two cuts on each loop
Open out bows

Thin Ribbon over wider Ribbon

Thin Ribbon over wider Ribbon

WRAPPING TRIMS

Berries
Ribbon

FLUFFY BOWS

These are the hallmark of the professional wrapper. Practice makes perfect, so take each step slowly and practise whenever you can.

☐ Use a 2 m length of satin sheen ribbon (2 cm wide).

☐ Unwind the ribbon, rewind 10 times around your hand, making sure there is no slack.

☐ Find the tail on top, and the tail inside. Make a fold halfway between these two. Press this end, and then the other end firmly.

☐ Keeping the index finger of your non-cutting hand tightly on the top left-hand edge, cut away a little more than one-third, in a triangle, from the other side.

☐ Turn ribbon over, and keeping your finger tight on the cut edge, cut away another piece (little more than a third), leaving a peninsula of only ⅛ in. This must be narrow for the bow to work. Do the same at the other end.

☐ Open the circle out and place both cut-away ends back together. Tie a tight double knot with a 12 in piece of thin ribbon of the same colour.

☐ Hold the tie and ends firmly. Take one loop at a time. Pull a single loop from the inside and twist it away from you firmly. Twist the next loop towards you. Make sure your fingers work in at the centre as you take each petal out. Take subsequent loops out following this sequence — one loop away and twist, one loop towards and twist. Do the same for the other untouched loop. You should have a ball of petals. (The key to success with fluffy bows is to have a tight narrow centre from which the petals of your 'rose' can be lifted and turned out.)

☐ To complete your fluffy bow, trim away ends, but not the tie. Lay your bow on the parcel, tie in place with a double knot, and turn the bottom row of petals over to sit nicely.

GIANT FLUFFY BOWS

Use 3 cm wide ribbon. Follow instructions as for fluffy bows, but use 2¾ m

of ribbon wrapped around your hand nine times. This needs a big loop, since the diameter of the loop gives the width of your final bow. If your hand is too small, cut a piece of heavy cardboard to the width you want, and wind ribbon round this tightly.

FLUFFY BOW

FLAT BOWS

☐ Take a piece of plain satin bow ribbon, 1 m long; cut off 15 cm for a separate tail.

☐ Make a circle 2 cm in diameter around your index finger, holding it in place with thumb.

☐ Make a loop at either side of the circle, slipping ribbon under your thumb.

☐ Make successive loops, slightly longer each time (you should make 3 loops either side and have a tail left on one side).

☐ Add your second tail underneath and use a tiny stapler, held upside down, to staple the bow in place.

☐ Trim ends to same length by pulling tails down under the bow, and cutting.

☐ Now fold both ends in half and cut at a 45 degree angle.

Note: To make two-colour bows, use ½ m of each colour ribbon and proceed as for flat bows.

THREE-COLOUR FLUFFY BOWS

These bows are especially good for Christmas and Christenings.

Use 1 m each of red, gold and green; or pink, blue and white, thin or wide

ribbon. Place on top of each other, then wind around your hand three times.

Follow instructions as for fluffy bows.

TWO-COLOUR BOWS

Use 1½ m of ribbon of each colour, place on top of each other, and then wrap five times round your hand. You now have the choice of mixing the two colours or having a 50/50 colour bow.

For a mixed colour bow, when you pull the loops out from the centre, pull two loops towards you, then two loops away from you.

For a 50/50 colour bow, which can become a rose, pull one loop away and one towards you, as with the basic fluffy bow. This will keep the two colours separate.

To make a rose, use two shades of a colour e.g. pink, follow the steps above, but at the end, turn the lighter colour petals to form the base of the rose, and use the darker colour for the centre.

LATTICE WRAP

This is ideal for a man's parcel, and any gift to be posted.

- ☐ Take three ribbons of different widths (these can be stripped to size) and colours or choose three shades of a colour.
- ☐ Arrange and then secure the first rows of ribbon under the parcel.
- ☐ Weave the first colour under, over, under and secure underneath.
- ☐ Do the same with the second and third ribbons, starting under then over.
- ☐ Secure all joins underneath with tape.

LATTICE WRAP

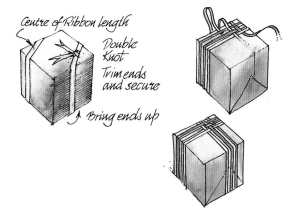

Centre of Ribbon length
Double Knot
Trim ends and secure
Bring ends up

TIE WRAP

This simple and attractive wrap looks best on rectangular boxes. Choose ribbon colours to match your paper or gift theme.

- ☐ Make a 'neck' with ribbon near the top of your parcel and secure it with rolled tape or double-sided tape under the parcel.
- ☐ Take two pieces of ribbon — one wide and one thinner. Cut them a little longer than the length of your box.
- ☐ Place one on top of the other then, holding the crossed section of the two ends, place the right side on top of the other right side to create a loop.
- ☐ Turn the loop over, and push these two ends under the neck you have made.
- ☐ Thread ends back through loop to make what is known in macrame as a *Larkshead knot*.
- ☐ Take ends down, trim to a point, and secure in place with tape.

TIE WRAP

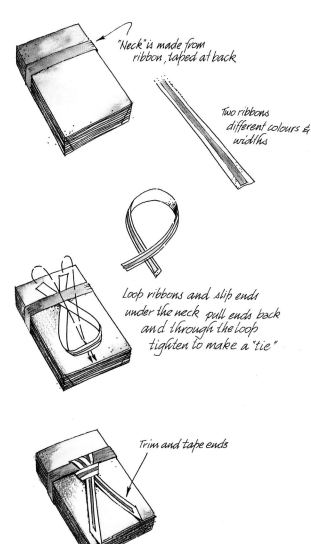

"Neck" is made from ribbon, taped at back

Two ribbons different colours & widths

Loop ribbons and slip ends under the neck pull ends back and through the loop tighten to make a "tie"

Trim and tape ends

SQUARE BOX WRAP

Find the centre of your wide wrapping ribbon and place this point over one corner. Take ribbons under the parcel and up to the opposite corner. Tie on top of the parcel with a simple double knot. Trim and secure the tails.

CHRISTMAS CARDS AND WRAPS

CARDS

Here are some simple ideas for making your own fabulous Christmas cards. In each case start off with a sheet of white, red or green card. Work out the sizes (check the size of your envelopes) and shapes you want (e.g. tree, bell), and cut out before decorating.

Potato print cards — Cut out the shape (e.g. holly, star) in relief on a well-drained potato half. Dip the cut area in coloured powder paint and stamp onto card. (Add glitter while paint is wet if you want that extra sparkle!)

Candle card — Draw a simple design on card using a wax candle. Paint over the top of your design with water-based paint. The wax image will stand out clearly from the coloured areas.

Bell card — Make a bell-shaped card and tie on small jingle bells with ribbon.

Concertina card — Fold a long strip of thin card like a concertina. Sketch a very simple shape on the front then cut out. Write a message inside (one word per fold).

Lace card — Place a paper doily over the card and scribble on doily with crayon to produce a lace pattern on the card.

Cut and stick card — Cut out a selection of bright, bold letters from magazines and stick on plain card.

Macaroni card — This card is fun for children to make. Glue macaroni shapes onto a large or small card and spraypaint with gold or silver paint. Alternatively spray the macaroni first and glue onto painted card.

Open Sesame card — Cut out two identical felt Christmas tree shapes 13 cm high and decorate.

Cut one tree in half lengthways. Fold a piece of card 30 cm × 20 cm to open in the centre. Stick one tree in the centre inside, and the two halves in identical positions on the outside opening. Open sesame!

FELT CHRISTMAS TREE NAPKIN HOLDERS

Materials: green felt, sequins, white wool

To make: Make paper templates of Christmas tree pieces (1), (2) and (3).
  Pin onto felt and cut shapes out.

Glue pieces (2) and (3) onto back of tree in positions marked.
  Sew or glue on sequins and strands of wool for snow. Use Slicker pens for other finishing touches.
  Fold paper napkin to fit securely under flap at the back of holder.

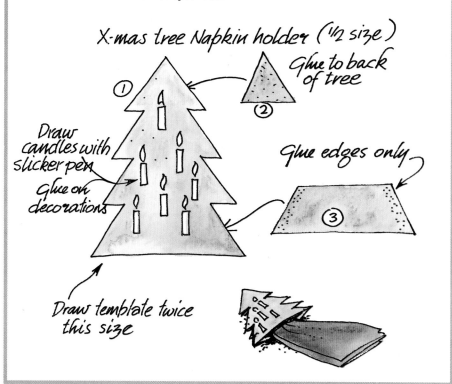

X-mas tree Napkin holder (1/2 size)

① Draw candles with Slicker pen. Glue on decorations

Glue to back of tree ②

Glue edges only ③

Draw template twice this size

shape on front same as shape inside

OPEN SESAME CARD (CHRISTMAS TREE)

18

Parterre Garden   Appley Hoare Antiques   Lois With Love

TINSELLED CHRISTMAS BOWS

Make a giant white fluffy bow. Cut ½ in pieces of silver tinsel and twist and staple to the top mid-point of each loop.

Tinsel can be used for your ties instead of ribbon. Multi-coloured tinsel also looks great on white bows.

WRAPPINGS

Decoration is traditionally an important part of the way we celebrate Christmas. Many of us not only decorate our Christmas tree, but also our front door, hearth and windows! Hospitality is essential to the occasion and our cheerful decorations welcome visitors and wish them well.

Giftwrapping Christmas presents is an equally important part of the festivities. The traditional colours are red, green, gold, silver and white. Gifts should be sashed with lots of ribbons using contrasting colours and different widths and lengths.

For those extra special touches use cut-out felt shapes (e.g. trees, bells, stars) as part of your wrapping.

Every year more opportunities for gift-giving seem to find their way into the calendar — relative newcomers like Mothers Day and Fathers Day are now jockeying for position with traditional events like Christmas and birthdays, but who's complaining?

While occasions like Easter and Valentines Day are steeped in folklore which often dictates the nature of gifts, newer celebrations on the scene often provide immense opportunity for original and inspired gestures.

2 THE CALENDAR OF GIFT GIVING

In this chapter, we hope you'll be fired up by some of our tips and suggestions to make any number of events throughout the year truly special occasions — you can make your own mark with wit and humour on April Fools Day with practical jokes specially geared to one person, or add a novel slant to traditional celebrations like Easter with a set of rabbit finger puppets, or a voucher offering 'eggs of your choice' for breakfast. Once the wheels are in motion, it's hard to stop such bright ideas popping into your head unbidden!

In celebrating this growing number of calendar events, we're often freed from the limitations that seem to accompany landmarks like a birthday, when a person counts on receiving a major item for their wardrobe or favourite hobby.

On Mothers Day, what mum wouldn't be thrilled with a cleverly contrived parcel of gifts? An all-white concoction of nightdress, soaps and towel, wrapped in glossy white paper and tied with lace or satin ribbon and topped with a bunch of white cyclamen is a terrific way to celebrate that special day!

Made Where   Mid City Granny May's Paper Shop   Mid City House and Garden   David Jones

NEW YEAR

The beginning of each new year has been celebrated for over 5000 years, even though it is only since 1762 that New Years Day has been on January 1. Our new year's resolutions actually originate in pagan promises made to the gods in exchange for good fortune.

New Year is celebrated in different ways around the world. In Scotland for instance, New Year's Eve is called Hogmanay, and the Scots spring-clean assiduously as part of the ritual of purification. Traditional foods eaten at this time are oatcakes, haggis, shortbread and scones.

In Greek communities, January 1 is called St Basil's Day. It's a day to visit friends and share a special cake called Vassilopitta, which conceals a silver or gold coin. The finder will have good fortune.

For lots of us, however, New Year is a time for parties, bell ringing, lots of noise, and a thoughtful, creative look ahead into the next year. The last year's problems fade away with the promise of a fresh batch of 365 days to work with.

THE PERSONAL TOUCH

✳ A house-cleaning package (with an explanatory note about the Scottish-Hogmanay traditional house clean). Fill a handy carry basket or bucket with cleaners, dusting cloths, soaps, and a symbolic twig brush to sweep in the New Year.

✳ Make a row of shortbread fingers (see recipe, p. 50), and tie a scrolled fortune to each biscuit.

✳ A 'Life-Changing' Book — It could be about getting organised, exercising, sensible diet, stress management, improving your golf swing, coming to terms with menopause, or learning the violin.

✳ New Year Voucher — Promise to paint a fence, make a kite, or go to the movies once a month. And keep your promise. Promise?

✳ Timely Gifts — A calendar; an alarm clock for a chronic late-riser; a diary.

✳ Enclose a set of very favourable fortunes in an ornate box, a new teapot, or a vase.

VALENTINES DAY

Love and romance, which we celebrate each February 14, has inspired some great words over the centuries. In more recent times the American poet, Louis Ginsberg, put it very well when he described love as 'the irresistible desire to be desired irresistibly'!

It's wonderful to indulge and be indulged and Valentines Day is a license for doing just that.

Valentines Day has a picturesque history dotted with star-crossed lovers and quaint romantic traditions. St Valentine, the patron Saint of lovers, was a third century Christian priest who was martyred on February 14 by Roman Emperor Claudius II for secretly marrying young lovers.

Valentines Day still essentially centres on romantic ideals and love. It's a day to be sentimental and to indulge your loved one. If the right romantic words are hard to come by, borrow a quotation from a famous lover or songwriter who has captured the mood of St Valentine.

Today the word 'Valentine' can mean a card, a gift or the person who is secretly or openly admired. Love-birds, cupid and arrows, roses, violets and hearts are the symbols commonly associated with St Valentines Day.

CLASSICS

Flowers — Long-stemmed red roses are acknowledged as the number one symbol of love. However, any pretty, fragrant flowers make beautiful gifts. Buy a single flower, a bunch, a bush, a corsage or a buttonhole using scented flowers — tuberoses, gardenias, jasmine, lavender, rose, tea rose, honeysuckle, daphne, or lilac. The quintessential Valentine flower is, of course, the forget-me-not.

Lingerie — Another Valentines classic! Whether you select a silk camisole, a pair of G-strings, pyjamas, a bath robe, black slip, satin sheets or a frivolous garter, make sure your wrapping is equally soft and sensuous.

Jewellery — A wonderfully romantic gift because of its small and often expensive nature. A tiny, exquisitely wrapped gift of jewellery — gold, silver or ceramic jewellery; pearls; diamonds; other precious and semi-precious stones — will always pass the test of time.

THE PERSONAL TOUCH

✳ Pink, red and white are popular colours for a collection of romantic gifts. Make up a gift of matching soaps, flannel, toiletries, drawer liners, potpourri, champagne, and a dainty posy wrapped in lots of pastel coloured tissue paper, ribbons and bows.

✳ Relabel a bottle of pink champagne with a romantic label tailored to your Valentine. Add two crystal flutes for a romantic toast if you're feeling extravagant!

✳ A romantic breakfast of croissants and champagne.

✳ A weekend away, at a classy city hotel, or a quiet country retreat.

✳ A 'common scents' voucher promising a luscious new fragrance, with the final choice made together.

✳ An 'Indulgence' voucher! Indulge your Valentine's every whim!

✳ Write your own romantic sonnet (a poem with 14 lines) or borrow one from one of the greats like Shakespeare. Present it on beautiful paper, scrolled and sashed with a red velvet ribbon.

✳ A 'Two's Company' voucher for a romantic dinner at home. Sample menu: artichoke hearts, beef chasseur, with heart-shaped croutons, followed by coeur a la creme, or classic crepe suzette. Serve your dinner in a subtle setting of soft music and candlelight. For fun, have a tiny gift hidden amongst the flowers.

✳ A tiny basket of heart-shaped chocolates or a heart-shaped chocolate cake presented with dazzling sparklers or a biscuit barrel of iced and decorated ginger heart biscuits (see recipe, p. 49)

✳ P.S. More Ideas — A pair of love birds (real or decorative); a romantic video (Gone With The Wind, Dr Zhivago), record, tape or CD; a blow-up print of your most flattering photo ; send a romantic telegram; fragrant drawer liners; a heart-shaped object e.g. a tin, cake tin, biscuit cutters, trinket box; a Lalique scent bottle, silver candlesticks, a music box or a loving cup; an initialled towel; writing paper with your initials entwined at the top; two brandy balloons and a bottle of liqueur.

Note: A pair of almost anything — where you each keep one — is a romantic Valentine gift.

EASTER

The word 'Easter' comes from *Eostre*, the name of an ancient pagan Goddess of Spring. Most modern day Easter traditions are an intertwining of ancient Northern hemisphere spring rituals of rebirth, featuring eggs, and the Christian celebration of the resurrection of Christ. It's interesting to note that eggs are also part of the Jewish Passover feast. And in Greece, red-coloured, hard-boiled eggs are offered to visitors on Easter morning, to symbolise the blood of Christ. With this backdrop, Easter eggs take on a deeper symbolic role. They represent birth and new life.

Because of their special role, eggs have been beautifully decorated and painted for Easter for thousands of years. In some countries it is a real art form.

We can continue that tradition by decorating eggs as well as eating the chocolate ones! Traditional Easter foods make excellent gifts and will be heartily enjoyed by all. Make a batch of hot cross buns, Easter eggs or kulich (a rich fruit bread). See recipes Chapter 4.

✳ Make a set of rabbit finger puppets for a child (see p. 58).

CLASSICS

An Easter without an egg would be like Christmas without Santa. Eggs, eggs and more eggs are the classic Easter gift, but you could add a dash of innovation and introduce the occasional papier-mâché, china or alabaster egg in the great tradition of Carl Fabergé, maker of bejewelled eggs for the Tsar of Russia. Start your own modest collection next Easter, or begin an egg cup collection using new and 'op'-shop cups for a different style each year.

For children, there are plenty of classic Easter stories and beautiful china. Best known perhaps are the Peter Rabbit stories of Beatrix Potter, and magical Bunnikins china. Bunnikins china is particularly collectable, and fun to give with an egg or two on the side.

THE PERSONAL TOUCH

✳ A colour coordinated parcel of flannels, teatowel, ribbons and buttons, wrapped in tissue, with more ribbons and some small toy chickens on top.

✳ Make up an egg decorating kit for children including paint brushes, non-toxic food colours, glitter, wool, flowers and glue. Add a book on how to decorate eggs (the Egg Marketing Board produces an excellent book on the subject).

✳ Make up a simple food hamper of delicious foods for an Easter picnic (see Chapter 4 for ideas).

✳ Make an Easter gift box for children. Paint an egg carton yellow, and fill each space with a small gift or Easter egg. Add a small toy chicken and a wide yellow bow for the finishing touches.

✳ Make an Easter bonnet from a cane hat, adult or child's size. Buy a selection of Easter treats (wrapped sweets and chocolates) and stitch on to the hat with double thread. Add a pretty bow of ribbon or lace.

✳ An Easter morning voucher could offer 'eggs of your choice' for breakfast. Offer a list of scrambled, fried, Benedict, and coddled.

✳ Have an Easter egg hunt on Easter morning. Write a light-hearted note from Eggbert the Easter Bunny, with clues in verse.

✳ Form marzipan into small egg shapes and decorate using food colours; or colour and decorate hard-boiled or blown eggs with non-toxic food colours and materials. (To blow an egg, pin prick both ends and blow the contents gently into a bowl. Rinse and dry.) Wrap eggs gently, as they are very fragile.

Appley Hoare Antiques,
Mid City Granny May's Paper Shop

APRIL FOOLS DAY

April Fools Day is THE day for nonsense, playing practical jokes and creating a harmless wave of infectious giggles. But how did such tomfoolery start?

The celebration of April Fools Day began in 1752 when the present Gregorian Calendar came into use. In the earlier Julian Calendar, the New Year began on March 25, and ended on April 1 with celebrations and gifts. When New Year changed to January 1, people kept up the tradition of giving gifts on April 1 but with a strong element of light-hearted fun.

April 1 has its own set of unique traditions. In France, anyone caught by a trick is called an April Fish or *poisson d'Avril*; in Scotland an April Fool is called a *gowk* or cuckoo. And in England, you need to be quick off the mark because April Fool jokes are only acceptable before lunch time, not after.

As far as gifts go, there are only rules to be broken! Anything goes, the sillier the better. But choose your victims carefully — a good sense of humour is essential.

MOTHERS DAY

The modern tradition of setting aside a special day for Mum to relax and enjoy began in the USA in 1914 when Anna Jarvis persuaded Philadelphians, and eventually Congress, to have a day to remember not just *her* mother, but all mothers.

Mothers have been worshipped in their own right for thousands of years, and celebrated by the Christian church on Mothering Sunday. In 18th century England, Mothering Sunday was a very special day when long suffering English servants were allowed the day off to visit their mothers, taking perhaps a traditional Simnel cake or a bunch of violets.

In modern times, the special colour we use for Mothers Day gifts and flowers is white, and the traditional flower has become the white chrysanthemum.

Mothers Day gifts, however, have changed over the last 20 years, and those old standbys of perfume, chocolates and jewellery have lost some popularity. Modern mums tend to be more particular about their diet and personal preferences.

Whatever the changes in fashion, the very best Mothers Day gifts always come from the heart. Think of your gift as acknowledging a mother's very special role in the family and in society. Take your time to choose; or make a very personal gift; or dream up a surprise outing or treat. Whatever you do, spend time, and lots of it, with your mother.

CLASSICS

For a touch of style, choose gifts which will stand the test of time e.g. fine glass, gold and silver, china, luxury linen, silk scarves, books and pen sets.

THE PERSONAL TOUCH

✹ Voucher — It could be for dinner at her favourite restaurant; a course of lessons e.g. tennis, piano, cookery, yoga, upholstery; a beauty treatment e.g. manicure, colour analysis, hair styling, facial; breakfast in bed for a week!

✹ A colour coordinated gift selection e.g. an all-white collection of nightdress, sweet-smelling soaps, and towel wrapped in tissue paper with lace and satin ribbon trimmings. Top with a bunch of white flowers or a delicate white cyclamen.

✹ Treat her to the movie or play of her choice.

✹ Tea Connoisseur's Kit — If your mother happens to be a dedicated tea drinker she will enjoy receiving some of the following items in a gift package: an array of bag and leaf teas (her favourites); new teas to try (scented, tisanes like camomile, herbal and green teas); a tea caddy; china tea cup and saucer; tray; cake plate; sugar bowl and milk jug; silver spoons; a teapot and cosy.

✹ Soap Lover's Kit — Find out what your soap lover's preferences are. If trying different soaps is a real passion, search out soap of all shapes, sizes, colours and perfumes from goat's milk and glycerine to tar and tea rose! Soaps can be presented beautifully wrapped in either cellophane or tissue paper and placed in a cane basket.

✹ Collector's Kit — People collect the strangest objects and if your mother enjoys collecting things, encourage her by starting a collection or contributing to one she already has. Her collection may be thimbles, antique china, bottles, glass or silver objects, vases or jugs to mention a few.

FATHERS DAY

Many women regard Fathers Day as one of the most difficult gift-giving occasions of the year. Men tend to be less overt about the kind of gifts they like and it's all too easy to rely on socks, jocks, aftershave and hankies — the old standbys! But Fathers Day doesn't have to be at all predictable, especially as most fathers have a variety of hobbies and interests which can be indulged.

According to the history books Fathers Day was first celebrated in America in 1909 by Mrs Sonora Dodd, whose widowed father had raised six children single-handed. The original idea of this special day was to encourage a better relationship between fathers and their children. In practice this means giving time and expression to your feelings.

CLASSICS

Fathers Day classic gifts tend to fall into quite a conservative category and the price range can vary considerably. The most important thing is to choose a gift which suits your father's personality and lifestyle, whether he is a bus driver, a gardener or an archaeologist!

What are his great loves in life? A classic gift for *your* father may be a selection of his favourite lures for trout fishing; for another father it may well be as simple as a box of chocolates! Attach a red or white rose to your gift for the perfect finish.

THE PERSONAL TOUCH

✻ Gift package made up of goodies which match your father's favourite hobby or highlight one of his more lovable foibles. If he is a keen golfer the package might consist of golfing gear like gloves, club covers, monogrammed tees, special socks and a related book or magazine.

✻ Service voucher for any jobs that need doing e.g. lawn mowing, car cleaning.

✻ Bunch of flowers made up of his favourites, or a house plant. If he likes or collects certain types of plants e.g. cacti, try to find a particular plant he's been chasing for a while — the rarer the better.

✻ Book or set of books — Find out what genre he enjoys (novel, thriller, horror, detective, western, action, romance).

✻ P.S. More Ideas — clock radio; shirt; T-shirt; night shirt; diary; chess or backgammon; lottery tickets; swiss knife; tie hanger; wine cooler; mug; tea cup and saucer; cuff links; tie pin; pen; brandy flask; leather gloves; toiletries bag; scarf.

CHRISTMAS

Christmas is a very special time for giving and receiving gifts. A time when we are all faced with the awesome task of choosing not one, but often dozens of gifts. No wonder New Year sees us all resolving to plan for next Christmas in July!

Christmas is a time for love and sharing, a time to be surrounded by family and friends. Every part is to be savoured — from the cooking smells and the icing on the Christmas cake to decorating the Christmas tree and carol singing.

CLASSICS

There are fewer specific Christmas classics, simply because of the grand scale of Christmas gift-giving. But almost any gift of quality that can be passed down through the family or savoured as the best of its kind, can be termed a Christmas classic.

For adults, that might include a bottle of fine old Scotch, a silk tie, a silver charm or bell, a Christmas anthology, a porcelain figurine, Christmas music, a time piece, a persian rug, perfume or gold jewellery.

For children, the same philosophy applies. Special Christmas china like Royal Doulton or Wedgwood will last for a future generation. So will a fine dictionary, quality jewellery, or classic literature. Classics like *Alice in Wonderland*, *Winnie the Pooh*, *Barbar*, *Treasure Island*, *Wind in the Willows*, *The Tale of Peter Rabbit*, *Heidi*, *Robinson Crusoe* have seen generations of readers. They are still very popular, as are modern classics, like *Spot's First Christmas*, or Jan Pienkowski's *Christmas*, which will still be read in 20 years time.

Special Christmas music is always a welcome gift, especially for those with a passion for carols; popular classics like Jingle Bells, White Christmas, I Saw Mummy Kissing Santa Claus; or traditional music like Handel's Messiah, J. S. Bach's Christmas Oratorio.

THE PERSONAL TOUCH

Almost any kind of gift parcel is acceptable at Christmas, so check the gift suggestions throughout the book for more ideas. Kits with a summery, outdoors theme are naturals for the holiday period.

✱ Beach or Holiday Kit — A range of practical items — suntan cream, beach towel, hat and beach mat, lip balm, insect repellent, deck chair, beach umbrella and sunglasses. Bundle everything up in a giant beach bag and rest assured your gift will get lots of use over the summer.

✱ Home-made gifts — Nothing is quite as special or personal, whether the end result is a tea cosy, handmade truffles, a woolly scarf, or a child's first home-made bookmark; it really is the thought that counts.

✱ Gourmet Food Parcels — The ideal gift for difficult people, the elderly and people who have everything. After all, they haven't got a jar of your special pickled onions, have they? Add your secret recipe of spices, cloves and sugar. A gourmet food parcel might include:

pates
herb vinegars
sauces (cranberry, tomato, fruit)
jams (apricot, cumquat, grapefruit marmalade)
jellies (apple, quince, ginger)
chutneys
mustards
biscuits (shortbread, melting moments, gingerbread)
herb butters
candied peel
brandied cherries
pickled onions
miniature Christmas cakes in brioche tins
mince pies
almond bread
German stollen (fruit log)
florentines
sweets (chocolate truffles, caramels, toffees, orange and lemon slices, marizpan, fruits)
petit fours
candied nuts
tiny puddings

For the finishing touches, buy some flavoured teas, peppermints, wine, mixed nuts in their shells, and mix these with home-made items. (Other finishing touches might include a wooden spoon, biscuit cutters, hand-written recipes, bundles of home-made bouquet garni, pine cones, holly napkins, cutlery, glasses or a cushion for picnics if appropriate.)

Small cellophane bags make ideal wraps, decorated with home-made card labels. Use small circles of lace fabric, small red sacks, or calico to add colour and interest to the parcel. Scrunched-up clear cellophane or straw makes excellent padding to fill out your parcel.

✳ Christmas Crackers — A box of stylish home-made Christmas crackers is an easy-to-make gift especially if the contents are good quality knick knacks rather than throwaways.

Here's how:
Cut up a kitchen roll cylinder into 11 cm lengths. Score in the middle of each cylinder so that they will break when bent.

Wrap your tiny gifts in tissue paper and place inside cylinders. Now wrap with 28 cm widths of shiny paper, frill the ends and tie with bows.

For the finishing touches glue on a band of threading broderie anglaise, lace or crepe paper. Add some kind of Christmas decoration, e.g. tie on some jingle bells, or cut-out felt Christmas shapes, and present laid out in a giftwrapped box. Just one, or six of these, if you're feeling more ambitious, make a spectacular Christmas gift.

✳ Tiny Tasty Tree — Break off a small branch from your Christmas tree or make a tree shape out of twigs or thin pieces of wood firmly bound together. Place standing up in a prepared box or pot. If necessary spray paint the branches of your 'tree', then decorate with the following: popcorn tinsel (made by threading onto cotton); gingerbread biscuits in an assortment of Christmas shapes (see recipe, p. 49) tied on with curling ribbon; jellybeans wrapped in cellophane bunches; candy walking sticks and other wrapped sweets.

✳ Advent Tree — Make a small 'tree' as above. Decorate with 25 giftwrapped matchboxes numbered 1–25, to be opened in the 25 days leading up to Christmas, one each day. The matchboxes should contain a variety of very small gift objects, e.g. coins, sweets, badges, jewellery, drawings and handwritten messages.

✳ Vanilla Sugar — Use an old jam jar with an interesting shape and fill it with white sugar. Add a whole vanilla bean; close, label and decorate with a pinked circle of Christmas or small print fabric. This is a simple, inexpensive and useful gift which children will enjoy making.

✳ Stocking Fillers — These tiny offerings can fill a space in a stocking or make a handy gift in their own right. Have plenty in your gift cupboard before Christmas in a box of their own marked 'small gifts'.

soap shapes
novelty
   toothbrushes
pencil cases
animal puppet
   gloves
small books
cassettes
notebooks
jigsaws
rubber insects
pirate's patch
pin cushions
tape measures
small paperbacks
cut-out dolls
tea towels
brooches
necklace and
   earrings
keyrings
magnets
notepads
badges
bathcubes
mirrors
stickers
farm animals
paint boxes
pens
packets of seeds
bangles
dice
pencil tops
stickers
hair clips
crayons
parasols
needle pack
laces
apron
stockings
nail polish
cosmetics purse
gloves
beads
nuts
nut crackers
sweets

✳ Christmas Plants — A small picea, a bonsai pine tree, a Norway spruce, or a Norfolk Island pine decorated with huge bows make attractive and lasting Christmas gifts. Other good Christmas plants include the native Christmas bush, cuphea (cigar bush); a Christmas rose (Helleborus); a pair of potted pines; a Christmas cactus and a native bursaria (Tasmanian Christmas Tree). Christmas lilies, red gloxinias, begonias or balsam all make beautiful gifts. (See Chapter 3 for more ideas.)

✳ Gifts for Unexpected Guests — It's lovely to have a small gift handy for Christmas visitors, young or old. Have a basket brimming with brightly wrapped soaps, nougats, bath salts, herb sachets, sweets and biscuits near your tree or have them hanging on the tree ready to be cut off. (Also see *Stocking Fillers*.)

Mid City Granny May's Paper Shop

Flowers are a gift that can never fail, but too often we expect an awful lot from a tired-looking bunch of limply-wrapped carnations!

Take the time to choose blooms which you know are special favourites, or put together a bunch that will complement a home decorative scheme. Sweet-smelling flowers like freesia or roses can waft their scent through an entire house but, if the person you are giving them to is unlikely to be at home much, a dried arrangement can make a far longer lasting alternative, as can a thoughtfully chosen houseplant.

3 SAY IT WITH FLOWERS

Houseplants can be as varied in size, shape, style and colour range as cut flowers, but have the additional charm of making a really longterm statement. A pot plant can make a highly effective contribution to the style of a room and there is a type to suit every sort of person . . . as well as all budgets! A flowering plant creates a welcome splash of colour, while the many and varied hues of variegated greenery make a soothing and delicate contrast. For the haphazard or forgetful plant enthusiast, a bowlful of cacti makes an attractive, no-fuss gift, while a fast-growing *impatiens* soon turns a small gesture into a large one!

The many hobbies associated with flowers and plants can provide great inspiration for gifts — what could be more helpful to the keen gardener than a set of top quality tools, or simply a set of excellent secateurs? Accessories like a stock of oasis, chicken wire, cut flower preservative or an unusual and attractive vase are perfect for the enthusiastic flower arranger.

Making a gift of flowers or plants provides endless opportunity to tailor your choice to the taste and style of the recipient — the sensory pleasure alone that they provide makes them a highly personalised present.

Parterre Garden   Mid City House and Garden   Mid City Granny May's Paper Shop   Lois With Love

GIVING FLOWERS

Flowers can be a fabulous gift — delightful to look at and to smell. They are often expected to do a huge gift job, with minimal effort on the giver's part. Six red carnations squashed together unimaginatively in pale green, wet tissue can look a little disappointing. Here are some tips for beautifully presented floral gifts.

- Avoid wayside flower sellers unless you're in a hurry. Find a florist who is willing to personalise your floral gift by making up the selection of colours and flowers you want.
- Always add your own wrapping paper to an arrangement. Silver paper, cellophane, or coloured tissue paper can complement most flowers.
- For special occasions combine more than one bunch of flowers and create a sensational impact.
- Buy flowers and arrange in a clear plastic box with greenery and a giant wide ribbon bow on top. Spray flowers with a fine water mist before closing the box.
- Give one beautiful, exotic flower in preference to six ordinary ones, and present it with style, sashed with wide ribbon, a gift tag, and some thoughtful words.
- Make a posy of flowers or herbs from your garden. Start with a central flower like a rose bud, and work outwards with rings of daisies, alyssum, and geraniums. For the final layer, add a feathery texture like forget-me-nots, lavender or gypsophila. Band with florist's wire or a rubber band. Add a circle of leaves — geranium, violet or maidenhair fern, or spikes of lavender. Place in the centre of a white doily. Cover the stems with foil and wrap in clear cellophane, silver paper or tissue.

For a special finishing touch include tiny wrapped chocolates with ribbon flowers or a fabric butterfly.

A sweet-smelling herb posy can be made from sprigs of rosemary, lavender, mint, thyme and cinnamon sticks wired in place and arranged in a doily wrapping tied with ribbons and lace.

Polyanthus Primroses

Crocuses

Anna Lily

Impatiens

Camellia

Mid City House and Garden

Spring Crocuses

Bougainvillea

Begonia

A GIFT OF FLOWERS
Selected cut flowers for special floral arrangements, gift bouquets, posies and sprays

Spring and Summer

COMMON NAME	BOTANIC NAME	COLOUR	TREATMENT
Agapanthus, African lily	*Agapanthus praecox*	blue, white	dip stem ends in boiling water then cool water for several hours
Amaranthus	*Amaranthus hypochondriacus*	shades of red	dip stem ends in boiling water then cool water for several hours
Azalea	*Azalea hybrids*	pink, purple, white	cut on diagonal and split with secateurs to 3 cm up stem; leave in water for four hours; a spray with hair lacquer will help hold blossoms
Boronia	*Boronia hybrids*	shades of pink	cut on diagonal; dip ends in boiling water then cool water for several hours
Christmas Bells	*Blandfordia nobilis*	red and yellow mix	re-cut stems under water before arranging
Cornflower	*Centaurea cyanus*	shades of blue; also pink, white, crimson	see Christmas Bells
Daffodil, Jonquil, Narcissus	*Narcissus* cultivars	yellow, white	pick in bud; change water frequently
Dahlia	*Dahlia hybrids*	blue, pink	remove leaves for 15 cm from bottom; scald ends
Dianthus (Chinese Pink)	*Dianthus chinensis*	pink	dip ends in boiling water for 30 seconds then plunge in cool water for several hours; sugar in the water helps prevent petals from falling
Floss Flower	*Ageratum houstonianum*	blue, pink, white	no treatment necessary; use in small arrangements
Foxglove	*Digitalis purpurea*	mauve, pink, cream, white, mixed	see Dianthus
Freesia	*Freesia x hybrida*	pink, apricot, blue, cream, white	cut on diagonal; give deep drink before arranging
Gardenia	*Gardenia augusta*	cream, white	store in damp paper or refrigerate in airtight box; never spray or touch petals
Geranium	*Geranium* x 'Johnson's Blue'	pink, mauve, blue	no treatment necessary; do not submerge foliage
Gypsophila	*Gypsophila elegans*	white	clean away foliage; re-cut and soak
Hydrangea	*Hydrangea macrophylla*	pink, blue, mauve, white	young heads will not last; cut mature heads only; strip leaves 25 cm up stem; scald and plunge in water overnight. Alum added to the water helps flowers to last
Iris	*Iris hybrids*	purple, pink, yellow, brown, white, mixed	re-cut stems under water; scald; change water frequently

Larkspur	Delphinium ajacis	blue, white, pink, mauve (pastel shades)	dip ends in boiling water for 30 seconds then plunge in cool water for several hours; sugar in the water helps prevent petals from falling
Lilac	Syringa vulgaris	pink, lilac, white	plunge in cool water, hammer and scald
Lily	Lilium hybrids	pink, yellow, white, red, speckled	see Agapanthus
Lupin	Lupinus hybrid	white, yellow, orange, purple, red, blue, pink	strip foliage from base of stem, scald and plunge into cool water for several hours
Marigold	Tagetes erecta	yellow, orange, gold	strip all foliage
Michaelmas or Easter daisy	Aster amellus 'Eventide'	blue, mauve, pink, crimson, white, yellow	remove most of foliage; heads may need to be supported with wire
Nasturtium	Tropaeolium major	yellow, orange, red	scald and soak in deep water; wire stems for support
Poppy	Papaver naudicaule	pink, red, yellow, orange, white	burn ends over open flame, leave in cool water for several hours
Ranuncula	Ranunculus asiaticus	yellow, orange, red, white	see Amaranthus
Rose	Rosa cultivars	pink, lilac, red, yellow, orange, white	remove thorns, cut on diagonal and scrape lower 8 cm of stem; scald; re-cut stems under water to revive
Shasta daisy	Chrysanthemum maximum	white with yellow centre	see Lupin
Snapdragon	Antirrhinum majus	red, yellow, orange, white	split ends and cut slightly on the diagonal
Statice	Limonium sp.	pink, mauve, blue, white, yellow	no treatment necessary; hang upside down to dry for use in winter arrangements
Stock	Mathiola incana	pink, lavender, purple, cream, white	see Lupin
Tuberose	Polianthes tuberosa	white, creamy yellow	strip foliage, cut on diagonal; pinch out centre buds so plant continues to develop
Tulip	Tulipa cultivars	pink, red, orange, yellow, white	push wire up stem, wrap in paper and place in deep water; re-cut before using.
Violet	Viola odorata	pink, purple, white	scald stems; dunk flower heads in water before arranging
Waratah	Telopea speciossima	red	bash stems

COMMON NAME	BOTANIC NAME	COLOUR	TREATMENT
Camellia	*Camellia japonica*	pink, red, white	see Gardenia
Carnation	*Dianthus caryophyllus*	pink, red, yellow, white, striped	cut between notches if possible; slit stem lengthways with secateurs
Chrysanthemum	*Chrysanthemum morifolium*	pink, purple, yellow, rust, white	see Lupin
Cineraria	*Senecio cruentus*	red, blue, purple	see Amaranthus; cut out damaged blooms from head
Gerbera	*Gerbera jamesonii*	yellow, red	see Amaranthus
Gladioli	*Gladiolus* hybrids	pink, red, yellow, white, mixed	break off two or three buds at top so other flowers will open; re-cut stems and place in warm water to open flowers
Orchid	*Dendrobium* variety	pink, white, yellow	avoid sprinkling blossoms as this will bruise petals
Pansy	*Viola x wittrockiana*	yellow, purple, brown, pink, mixed	cut stems with sharp knife
Poinsettia	*Euphorbia pulcherrima*	red	burn stem over open flame; remove leaves and burn remaining scars; leave in cool, deep water to condition
Sweet pea	*Lathyrus odorata*	pink, red, mauve, purple, white	scald in boiling water and leave in cool water overnight
Watsonia (Bugle lily)	*Watsonia* hybrid	white, pink, mauve	see Amaranthus

HOUSEPLANTS

Houseplants make terrific gifts, and last for much longer than a bunch of flowers. There are a whole range of accessories which can be part of the gift too, from a terracotta pot to a bag of repotting mix!

Maidenhair Fern

Cyclamen

Chamaedarea elegans

GIFTS FOR THE GARDENER

Whether your gardener loves growing flowers or vegetables; landscape gardening or simply pottering, there is a wonderful gift range to choose from. Find out what they need or would really like — it could be a new wheelbarrow or a packet of rare seeds!

Codiaeum

You don't have to be a picky gourmet or even a greedy gourmand to enjoy food as a present — we all have our favourite fancies, whether it's home-made shortbread or a jar of best caviar!

There are endless occasions traditionally celebrated with a feast or special foods like hot cross buns and chocolate eggs at Easter and mince pies at Christmas. You can put your own stamp on these events by presenting food offerings with a difference — for instance, packing a yuletide hamper with beautiful goodies like mince pies, pate, stuffings and sauces, pickles and preserves and a fruitcake you've baked and iced yourself or an Easter basket crammed with home-baked hot cross buns, kulich, and hand-decorated eggs.

4 FOOD WONDERFUL FOOD

Giving someone their favourite mouthwatering morsel is always an inspired idea, especially if you can make it a surprise — when a great aunt nostalgically mentions a passion for lemon curd, imagine her delight at receiving a jar you've prepared yourself for Christmas!

Sweets and chocolates provide an excellent safety net on most gift-giving occasions and instead of the usual cellophane-wrapped box of chocs from the corner shop, try making your own bonbons or give a selection of Continental chocolates, daintily gift-wrapped to make a memorable gesture.

Everyone loves a present that is personalised whether it's an extra special cake or a simple jar of home-made jam. By giving a little thought to the recipient's hobbies and habits, you're bound to come up with the right idea!

Lois With Love   Mid City House and Garden   Appley Hoare Antiques   Mid City Granny May's Paper Shop

SPECIAL OCCASIONS

CROQUEMBOUCHE

1 quantity Choux Pastry (see recipe)	**2** tablespoons Grand Marnier
FILLING	**2** teaspoons grated orange rind
3 cups thickened (double) cream	**2** quantities Spun Sugar (see recipe)
½ cup icing sugar	

Drop slightly rounded teaspoons of choux mixture onto a greased baking tray about 5 cm apart. Bake at 200°C (400°F) for 10 minutes. Reduce temperature to 180°C (350°F) and bake a further 15–20 minutes or until well puffed and golden brown.

Remove from oven, make a small slit in the side of each puff to allow steam to escape. Return puffs to oven for a few minutes to dry out and cool completely. Repeat with remaining pastry until all is finished.

Make a small hole in the base of each puff and pipe in a little filling.

Place Croquembouche cone on a plate. Dip each puff into caramel mixture for Spun Sugar and arrange the cone, joining the puffs together as you go.

Decorate Croquembouche with remaining Spun Sugar.

Serve within 6 hours or the puffs will soften.

To make filling, whip cream and icing sugar together to form soft peaks. Fold in Grand Marnier and orange rind.
Note: To make a tall Croquembouche you will need a Croquembouche cone. This adds support and helps the dessert to keep for hours. The cones are available from kitchenware stores.

Serves 6

CHOUX PASTRY
Pate a choux

⅔ cup flour	**75** g butter
⅔ cup water	**3–4** eggs, slightly beaten
pinch salt	

Sift flour onto a piece of greaseproof paper. In a saucepan heat water, salt and butter until butter is melted. Remove pan from heat and add all flour at once. Beat vigorously with a wooden spoon until mixture is smooth. Return pan to low heat and beat until mixture pulls away from sides of pan to form a ball. Cool to tepid.

Beat in eggs, a little at a time, beating well between each addition. The mixture should be glossy and hold its shape when dropped from the spoon. Use as required.
Note: All the egg may not be needed. The mixture will not hold its shape if too much egg is added.

Makes sufficient dough to line 1 × 20 cm flan tin.

SPUN SUGAR

1 cup caster sugar	**½** cup water
pinch cream of tartar	

Combine all ingredients in a small saucepan and heat gently stirring until the sugar dissolves. Using a wet pastry brush, brush away any remaining crystals from the side of the pan as these will cause the syrup to crystallise.

Increase the heat and boil until a rich golden colour. Allow to cool slightly. Working over sheets of baking paper, dip two forks into the syrup, join together then draw apart to form fine threads of toffee. Work quickly before the toffee sets and remember that it is very hot. When all the toffee has been used carefully lift the threads from the paper and place a little on top of each caramel custard.

COEUR A LA CREME

375 g cream-style cottage cheese	**1** punnet raspberries or **250** g frozen, thawed
250 g cream cheese	**1** punnet fresh strawberries, for garnish
1 tablespoon icing sugar, sifted	
¼ cup thickened cream (double cream), whipped	

Cream together the 2 cheeses and fold in icing sugar and whipped cream. Line 6 Coeur a la Creme moulds with muslin and stand on a small tray. Spoon cheese mixture into moulds, smooth top and refrigerate overnight.

Unmould onto 6 dessert plates and remove muslin. Sift icing sugar over the top.

To make raspberry sauce, blend raspberries in processor. Sweeten to taste with icing sugar if desired. Spoon sauce around each Coeur a la Creme, placing strawberries to one side.

Note: Coeur a la Creme moulds are white, heart-shaped moulds available from cookware and department stores in the gourmet cookware section. Small ramekin moulds may be used as a substitute.

PEAR AND CHOCOLATE SPONGE

175 g butter or margarine	**CHOCOLATE BUTTERCREAM**
175 g caster sugar	**225** g icing sugar
3 eggs	**225** g butter
175 g self-raising flour	**4** teaspoons cocoa powder
4 tablespoons chopped walnuts	few drops vanilla essence
12 canned pear halves, drained	
7 walnut halves	

Preheat oven to 190°C (375°F).

Cream fat and caster sugar until light and fluffy, then beat in eggs, one at a time, adding a spoonful of flour with each. Sieve remaining flour and fold in with a metal spoon.

Divide mixture between two greased and lined 20 cm sandwich tins. Bake for 25–30 minutes. Turn out and cool on a wire rack.

To make chocolate buttercream: sieve icing sugar and beat with butter until light and fluffy. Blend cocoa powder with a little boiling water, and stir into butter and sugar with a few drops of vanilla essence.

Split each sponge in half. Spread 3 of them with ½ the buttercream. Lay 6 pear halves on top of buttercream. Sandwich together, with plain sponge on top.

Spread top and sides of cake with buttercream. Press chopped nuts on to sides. Arrange remaining 6 pear halves over top and drizzle with chocolate. Decorate with walnut halves.

Serves 8

THEME BIRTHDAY CAKES

VICTORIA SANDWICH

125 g butter	**1** cup self-raising flour
½ cup caster sugar	**3** tablespoons jam
2 eggs	icing sugar

Preheat oven to 175°C (340°F). Cream butter and sugar until soft. Whisk eggs, beat into sugar mixture. Fold in flour. Spoon mixture into 2 greased and lined 15 cm sponge tins. Bake for 20 minutes. Remove cakes from tins and cool on cake rack.

Spread jam onto first cake and sandwich to second. Sprinkle top with icing sugar or ice and decorate as a birthday cake.

Serving Suggestions: Try decorating your cake with some of the following: flowers, small toys, marzipan miniature fruits, smarties, jaffas or other sweets, hundreds and thousands, glace fruits, silver balls, whipped cream, sliced fresh fruit, candles and anything else that appeals to your imagination. Boys or athletic girls may like a cricket cake: use green icing for grass, desiccated coconut for the pitch, candles for stumps, a jaffa for a ball and small dolls to represent players. Girls may like heart-shaped cakes with plenty of fancy icing decorations. Try using different shaped tins — there is plenty of variety available.

NUMBER CAKE

3 litres ice cream

Have a cake board or tray big enough to take 2 blocks of ice cream across and 6 along its length (each block being 500 mL).

Soften the ice cream by leaving it for 30 minutes in the refrigerator.

With a palette knife dipped in hot water, smooth the sides of the iced blocks and push together. Smooth the top and outsides of the total mass.

Freeze for 30 minutes.

Etch the shape of the number required on the block. Dip the knife in hot water again and cut the figure out.

Smooth over the figure and return to freezer.

Soften the leftover ice cream and place back in a container.

Serving Suggestion: Decorate with whipped cream and fresh fruit; coat with chocolate.

Serves 8

THE GINGERBREAD LOG CABIN

1 kg thick honey	**ICING**
1 cup water	**2 egg whites**
5 cups rye flour	**3 cups icing sugar**
3½ cups wholemeal flour	**1 tablespoon lemon juice**
1 cup chopped mixed peel	
1 teaspoon ginger	**DECORATION**
1 teaspoon cinnamon	glace cherries
½ teaspoon nutmeg	blanched almonds
1 teaspoon bicarbonate of	sweets
soda	plastic toy trees and
	people

Bring honey and water to boil in a saucepan, stirring continuously. Leave to cool.

Sift flours and add mixed peel, spices and bicarbonate. Make well in centre and add honey mixture. Blend mixture into a soft dough. Refrigerate dough wrapped in plastic wrap overnight.

Divide dough into 6 equal portions. If dough is too stiff set aside in a warm place for 15 minutes until easy to handle.

To make roof, roll out 2 portions to 6 mm thickness and 20 cm square. Set aside on lightly greased tray and prick with a fork.

To make walls, use 3 portions of dough and roll into sausage shapes about 1 cm in diameter.

The 4 walls require a total of:
  28 logs 20 cm long
  4 logs 19 cm long
  2 logs 16.5 cm long
  2 logs 12.5 cm long
  2 logs 10 cm long

To make each end wall, place on lightly greased tray side by side:
  7 × 20 cm logs
  1 × 19 cm log
  1 × 16.5 cm log
  1 × 14 cm log
  1 × 12.5 cm log
  1 × 10 cm log

To make remaining 2 walls, place on a greased tray side by side:
  7 × 20 cm logs
  1 × 19 cm log

Preheat oven to 200°C (400°F). Bake roof 12–18 minutes then cool on cake rack. Leaving 2 mm gap between each log, bake each wall 12–18 minutes. During baking, the gaps close to form the wall. Allow to cool on rack.

From 1 wall cut out:
  1 door 2.5 × 6.5 cm
  1 window 4 × 2.5 cm

With remaining dough, make:
  4 logs 2.5 cm long and 1.2 cm thick.

On baking tray place 2 logs next to each other and 2 logs on top to make double layer — this forms the chimney.

Knead remaining uncooked dough. Roll into flat 6 mm thick square 22 × 22 cm. This will form the base of the house. Prick with fork. Place on tray with chimney logs and bake 12–18 minutes. Cool on cake rack.

Whisk egg whites and fold in icing sugar to form smooth paste. Add lemon juice.

Place base on board or tray. Using icing, join 4 walls together at corners on top of base. Allow to dry completely at each stage of construction. Join roof to house with icing.

Thin 3 tablespoons of icing with a few drops of water. Gently drizzle icing over roof to resemble snow. Attach chimney to roof.

Divide window cut out in half. Place each half on either side of window to resemble shutters and attach with icing. Decorate house and garden with icing, cherries, nuts, sweets and plastic toys. Allow to set completely.

1 Make 2 walls and 2 end walls
2 Join walls
3 Join roof to house with icing
4 Drizzle icing over roof to make snow

CHOCOLATE DELIGHTS

Cooking with Chocolate

- When a recipe requires melted chocolate, it must be heated in a bowl or on a plate suspended over (but definitely not in) a pan of hot, but not boiling, water. Overheated chocolate has a bitter taste and loses its glossy shine and delicious aroma.
- Melt chocolate slowly without stirring, although some cooks advocate working it with a palette knife if it is to be used for coating cakes or making chocolate cases because that helps to keep the gloss when it sets. The chocolate should be no more than lukewarm.
- Chop or break chocolate into small pieces before melting so it melts quickly and evenly. Do not stir chocolate while it melts.
- Test that chocolate is melted by dipping the point of a knife into the centre.
- Cool chocolate at room temperature because this also helps to maintain the gloss.
- Be careful that not even a drop of water gets into the bowl (unless this is part of the recipe). Water prevents a good sheen and will make the chocolate thick.
- Remember that drinking chocolate and cocoa are not interchangeable: drinking chocolate has a milder, sweeter flavour.
- Handmade chocolates are best when eaten fresh. Most will keep well for 2–3 weeks.
- Do not refrigerate handmade chocolates or they will discolour and will sweat when you remove them from fridge.

HAZELNUT TRUFFLES

250 g dark compound chocolate	**20–24** whole, roasted hazelnuts
½ cup thickened cream	**200 g** dark compound chocolate for dipping
1 teaspoon vanilla essence	
60 g chopped, unsalted, roasted hazelnuts	

Chop chocolate and put in bowl over hot water, stirring occasionally until melted. Place cream in saucepan on stove and bring to boil, stirring constantly.

Remove cream from stove and cool to room temperature. Add cream and vanilla essence to melted, cooled chocolate and allow mixture to stand for about ½ hour. Beat with electric mixer until mixture is fluffy and lighter in colour.

Fold in chopped hazelnuts and refrigerate for ½ hour. Roll mixture into balls around each hazelnut and place on lined tray.

Melt additional chocolate by standard method, coat truffles and allow to set on tray. Alternatively, sandwich truffles between moulded shells, or use truffle to fill chocolate moulds.

PASSIONFRUIT CREAMS

200 g *condensed milk*	**150 g** *dark or white*
2 *passionfruit*	*compound chocolate*
500 g *icing sugar*	

Combine condensed milk, passionfruit pulp and 400 g icing sugar and mix well to form a firm dough. On a board, thoroughly knead mixture into remaining icing sugar. If mixture is not firm enough to roll into balls, add more icing sugar.

Roll into small balls (big enough to fit into chocolate cases) and refrigerate for ½ hour.

Melt chocolate and use to coat foil cases or moulds. Refrigerate until set. If using foil cases, remove them from chocolate when set. Place passionfruit balls into chocolate cases or moulds and refrigerate.

CHOCOLATE MOULDING

Solid Chocolates

1. Moulds must be clean and dry.
2. Fill mould with melted chocolate and tap on table to remove air bubbles.
3. Chill mould in freezer until set (about 3 minutes).
4. Tap mould gently to remove chocolates.

Filled Chocolates

1. Quarter fill the mould with melted chocolate and tap to remove air bubbles.
2. Brush chocolate evenly up the sides of the mould to make a shell and freeze until set (approximately 2 minutes).
3. Add filling such as truffle, nuts, fondant, fruit, etc.
4. Fill to top with melted chocolate and tap gently to remove air bubbles.
5. Return to freezer to set (about 3 minutes), remove and gently tap out chocolates.

Marbled Chocolates

1. Spoon a little white and dark chocolate separately into dish.
2. With a teaspoon swirl the white into the dark chocolate to make marble patterns.
3. Gently scoop up chocolate and fill mould evenly.
4. Tap to remove air bubbles and freeze until set (about 3 minutes). Then tap out chocolates.

Note: 250 g compound chocolate makes 25–30 chocolate shells or 10–20 whole chocolates, depending on the size of the mould.

EASTER FAVOURITES

HOT CROSS BUNS

2 cups flour	¼ teaspoon nutmeg
2 cups wholemeal flour	½ teaspoon allspice
1 teaspoon salt	
30 g dry yeast	**CROSS**
1½ cups warm milk	½ cup flour
¼ cup sugar	⅓ cup water
½ cup sultanas	
60 g butter, melted	**GLAZE**
1 egg	2 tablespoons sugar
¼ teaspoon cinnamon	1 tablespoon gelatine
	2 tablespoons hot water

Sift flours and salt into a bowl. Cream yeast with ½ cup warm milk and 1 teaspoon sugar. Make well in centre of flour. Add milk and yeast. Sprinkle flour over top, cover bowl with plastic wrap and stand in warm place 10 minutes until mixture bubbles.

Blend together remaining milk, sultanas, butter, sugar, egg and spices. Combine flour mixture with milk and sultana mixture. Blend evenly to form dough.

Knead on floured board 10 minutes. Place dough in oiled bowl. Cover with plastic wrap. Stand in warm place 40 minutes or until dough doubles in bulk.

Punch down dough, turn onto floured surface. Knead dough till smooth. Divide dough into thirds, then cut each third into 5 equal portions. Knead each into round shape. Place buns in lightly greased 18 x 28 cm lamington tin. Cover and stand in warm place 10 minutes or until buns reach top of tin. Preheat oven to 220°C (400°F).

Combine flour and water to make crosses. Place in corner of plastic freezer bag. Snip corner from bag. Carefully pipe crosses on each bun. Bake for 15–20 minutes. Remove from oven and brush with glaze. Cool buns on cake rack.

To make glaze, place sugar, gelatine and water in small saucepan. Bring to boil. Boil 1 minute.

Makes 15 buns

CHOCOLATE EASTER EGGS

chocolate (see note)	**ROYAL ICING**
	1 egg white, stiffly beaten
FONDANT	200 g icing sugar, sifted
2 teaspoons gelatine	few drops colouring
1 tablespoon water	(optional)
1 teaspoon liquid glucose	
or sweetener	
450 g icing sugar	

Making Easter eggs will require an egg mould, piping nozzles and bag, a paint brush and aluminium foil.

Melt chocolate in a bowl over hot water. Using a paint brush, cover the sides of your egg mould completely with melted chocolate. Chill in refrigerator 2 minutes.

Recoat mould with chocolate 3 times, so that chocolate forms a layer 2 mm thick. Chill between coats so chocolate sets.

Push top of mould gently to remove chocolate from mould and set egg halves on a piece of aluminium foil. Join egg halves with a little melted chocolate; chill in refrigerator 10 minutes to set.

To make fondant, soak gelatine in water, dissolve over heat and combine with glucose. Gradually add half the icing sugar, wrap in plastic wrap and set aside for 3 hours. Before using, add remaining icing sugar and colouring if desired. Make ornamental leaves and flowers and place on top of egg.

To make icing, fold beaten egg white into icing sugar with colouring, if desired, and beat well until stiff. Pipe decorations around and on top of egg.

Note: Quantity of chocolate depends on size of moulds and number of eggs required.

KULICH

40–50 g yeast	**50 g almond meal**
1½ cups warm milk	**5–6 ground cardamom**
1 kg flour, sifted	**seeds**
½ teaspoon salt	**¼ teaspoon nutmeg**
6 eggs	**¼ teaspoon cinnamon**
1½ cups sugar	**½ teaspoon powdered**
300 g butter	**saffron**
200 g raisins	**½ teaspoon vanilla**
50 g candied peel, finely	**essence or vanilla pod**
chopped	

In a large mixing bowl, dissolve yeast in warm milk, stir in half the flour and mix till smooth. Cover with a cloth to rise. When dough has doubled, add salt, egg yolks, leaving a small amount to brush the top. Add sugar and butter. Mix well. Beat egg whites till stiff and fold into the mixture alternately with remaining flour. Continue mixing until the dough can be formed into a ball and does not stick to the sides of the bowl. Cover and set aside. When dough has again doubled add raisins, candied peel, almond meal, spices and vanilla. Mix very well. It is traditional to serve a kulich with a pink rose.

The dough should be baked in tins which are round and tall. The height should be greater than the diameter. Old tin canisters are ideal, 15–20 cm diameter and 25–30 cm tall.

Butter pieces of greaseproof paper on both sides and line bottom and sides of tin allowing paper to protrude up to 4–5 cm above the tin.

Fill the tin about one-third full. Cover and set aside. When the dough has risen to about three-quarters full (which should take about 30 minutes), brush top with beaten egg. Preheat the oven to 180°C (350°F) and bake for 50–60 minutes. The top will rise over the tin like a mushroom. If it begins to burn, cover top with the same paper used for lining the tin.

When ready, the kulich should be a golden colour. Test with a straw. If it comes out clean, the kulich is cooked. Remove from oven and let stand for 5 minutes to cool. Place tin on its side and pull the paper lining. Paper and kulich should emerge easily. Place it upright on a cake rack to cool.

This recipe should make 2 large kulich. Smaller ones are traditionally given as gifts. Use tin from canned fruit or coffee. Remove the paper labels and check that container is safe to heat. Cook smaller kulich 40–50 minutes or until golden brown.

TRADITIONAL KULICH ICING

1 piece clean muslin or	**2 egg whites, beaten until**
cotton 20–25 cm square	**very stiff**
2 cups icing sugar	**1 teaspoon strained lemon**
	juice

Arrange muslin square on a cold flat surface. Mix icing sugar with egg whites and lemon juice.

With a wet knife working quickly, spread the mixture over the material thickly and evenly. Allow to settle for about 5 minutes then drape over the kulich. Often a cut-out border to give a lace effect is made. The top should set very hard. Take care not to crack the icing when removing muslin for serving. It should slide off mushroom top easily.

To serve, cut mushroom cap off kulich. Then cut crossways about 2 cm thick and then into quarters. The cap can then be replaced without obvious disturbance.

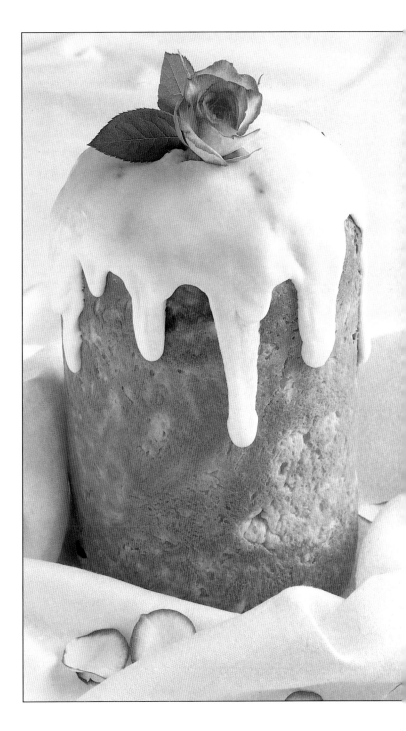

CHRISTMAS CHEER

ROAST TURKEY WITH HERB STUFFING

5–6 kg turkey

HERB STUFFING
185 g butter, melted
2 teaspoons salt
½ teaspoon fresh sage
½ teaspoon fresh thyme
pepper, to taste

4 cups soft bread cubes
¾ cup milk
2 stalks celery, chopped
1 small onion, chopped

BASTE
1/4 cup orange juice
60 g butter, melted

Rinse turkey and pat dry with paper towel.

To make herb stuffing, combine all ingredients in a large bowl, adjust seasoning to taste.

Fill turkey cavity with stuffing and sew or skewer openings. Secure drumsticks under skin at tail. Place, breast side up, on rack in roasting pan. Brush turkey with baste (orange juice and butter combined), cover with aluminium foil and bake at 175°C (340°F) for 3 hours.

Remove foil, baste again and continue cooking a further 30 minutes–1 hour to brown. Cover and allow turkey to stand 20 minutes before carving. Serve hot or cold.

Serves 12

CHRISTMAS MINCE PIES

PASTRY
2⅓ cups flour
1 teaspoon cinnamon
salt, to taste
180 g butter
½ cup caster sugar
1 egg, lightly beaten

FRUIT MINCE
1½ cups mixed dried fruit
440 g can crushed
  pineapple and juice

1 cooking apple, peeled,
  cored and grated
1 cup brown sugar
1 teaspoon nutmeg
1 tablespoon cornflour
  blended with 1
  tablespoon pineapple
  juice

Sift flour, cinnamon and salt into a bowl. Rub in butter to resemble breadcrumbs. Stir in sugar and egg to form dough. Knead lightly then wrap in plastic and refrigerate 1 hour. Grate half the dough over base of 30 x 20 cm lamington tin. Press down lightly and evenly with the back of a spoon. Set aside. Preheat oven to 180°C (350°F).

Place mixed fruit, pineapple and juice, apple, sugar and nutmeg in saucepan. Add cornflour paste and simmer until thickened. Cool slightly. Spread fruit mince over pastry base. Grate remaining dough over top to completely cover mince. Bake 35–40 minutes or until golden brown. Cool on wire rack. Cut into bars.

Makes 12–16

GRAN'S TRADITIONAL CHRISTMAS CAKE

500 g butter
2 cups brown sugar
10 eggs
1 cup glace cherries,
    chopped
½ cup mixed peel
3 cups sultanas
3½ cups currants
1½ cups raisins, chopped
½ tablespoon allspice
¼ cup rum
1 teaspoon vanilla
¼ cup milk
5 cups flour
½ tablespoon baking
    powder
	ALMOND PASTE
	1 cup ground almonds
	⅓ cup icing sugar
	¼ cup caster sugar
	1 egg white
	
	ICING
	2 egg whites
	500 g icing sugar
	1 teaspoon glycerine
	2 teaspoons lemon juice
	food colouring (optional)

Preheat oven to 160°C (325°F). Cream butter and sugar until smooth. Add eggs one at a time and beat mixture for 5 minutes. Add fruits, spice, rum, vanilla and milk. Lastly add sifted flour and baking powder and blend.

Spoon mixture into a double-lined 23 cm round or square cake tin. Carefully bang tin twice on benchtop to release air pockets from cake mix. Bake for 5–5½ hours. Insert wooden skewer to test if cake is cooked.

Stand on cake rack and cool cake in tin ½–1 hour before inverting onto cake rack to cool. Leave lining paper on cake. When cold, wrap in greaseproof paper and aluminium foil to store. Decorate cake with icing or Christmas fruit.

To make almond paste, blend together ground almonds and both sugars in a bowl. Stir in egg white and knead mixture to a smooth, thick paste. Dust a board with a little icing sugar and roll paste out to form a circle to fit top of cake.

To make icing, beat egg whites until frothy. Add sugar gradually, beating after each addition. Lastly add glycerine and lemon juice and beat for several minutes.

Divide icing, using white icing on top and sides of cake and colouring a small amount for decoration.

CHRISTMAS GINGERBREAD BISCUITS

125 g butter
3 tablespoons golden
    syrup
1 teaspoon bicarbonate
    soda dissolved in
    1 tablespoon boiling
      water
	50 g brown sugar
	250 g flour
	pinch of salt
	2 teaspoons ground ginger

Combine butter, sugar and golden syrup in a bowl and blend well until creamy. Add bicarbonate of soda then sifted dry ingredients.

Shape as desired using biscuit cutters or roll into small balls and flatten out with fork. Bake on greased oven trays for 20–30 minutes at 180°C (350°F).

When biscuits are cool make icing (see recipe) and decorate biscuits using a piping bag.

GINGER HEART BISCUITS

To make biscuits use the same ingredients and method as above but cut biscuits into heart shapes. Bake biscuits and when cool pipe icing around biscuit to accentuate heart shape.

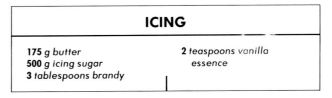

ICING

175 g butter **500** g icing sugar **3** tablespoons brandy	**2** teaspoons vanilla essence

To make icing, soften butter and blend with sifted icing sugar. Mix in brandy and vanilla essence and beat until creamy. This icing keeps well if refrigerated.

SWEET TREATS

OATY DATE SQUARES

*finely grated rind and juice of **1** orange*	*¾ cup brown sugar*
***1½** cups chopped dates*	*¾ cup rolled oats*
***100** g butter*	*½ cup wholemeal flour*

Make up orange juice to 100 mL with water. Cook dates and rind in orange water over low heat until soft and pulpy.

Blend butter and dry ingredients and press half into lightly greased 18 cm square tin. Spread date mixture over, top with remaining oat mixture and press down. Bake at 180°C (350°F) 35–40 minutes. Cool in tin then cut into 16 squares.

CAROB COOKIES

***150** g butter*	***2** cups self-raising flour*
¾ cup brown sugar	*½ cup raisins*
***1** egg*	*½ cup chopped walnuts*
¼ cup carob powder	

Cream butter and sugar, beat in egg then stir in remaining ingredients until well mixed. Roll into walnut-size balls and place on lightly greased baking sheet. Flatten lightly with fingertips or fork.

Bake at 180°C (350°F) 12–15 minutes. Cool on baking sheet 2–3 minutes then lift on to cake rack to cool completely.

Makes 45

SCOTCH SHORTBREAD

***125** g butter*	***1** egg, beaten*
***1⅛** cups flour*	***1** tablespoon cream*
¾ cup cornflour	*sugar for dusting*
¼ cup caster sugar	

Preheat oven to 180°C (350°F). Grease baking sheet. Rub butter into flour, until mixture resembles breadcrumbs. Add cornflour, sugar, egg and cream and mix to a stiff dough.

Roll dough out on a floured board to 1.75 cm thick, and cut into rounds with a 6 cm pastry cutter.

Arrange rounds on baking sheet. Prick each one with a fork and bake for 30 minutes. Dust with a little sugar and leave to cool.

Makes 15

FRUITY COCONUT BARS

½ cup wholemeal flour	*½ cup brown sugar*
***1½** teaspoons baking powder*	*½ cup sultanas*
½ teaspoon ground cinnamon	*½ cup chopped dried apricots*
¼ teaspoon ground ginger	***1** cup desiccated coconut*
⅛ teaspoon ground nutmeg	***2** eggs, beaten*
	***75** g butter, melted*
	***1** tablespoon milk*

Sift flour with baking powder and spices. Combine with sugar, fruit and coconut. Beat in eggs, butter and milk. Spread mixture in greased and lined 18 x 27 cm shallow tin and bake at 180°C (350°F) 30 minutes. Leave to cool in tin then cut into 16 bars.

HOME PRESERVES

PICKLED ONIONS

1 kg small white onions	**½ teaspoon** ground
450 g salt	allspice
2.25 litres water	**2 tablespoons** brown sugar
750 mL white vinegar	**2** whole gloves
250 mL tarragon vinegar	**1** cinnamon stick
1 tablespoon black	
peppercorns	

Wash unpeeled onions and place in a bowl. Mix half the salt with half the water and pour brine over onions to completely cover them. Weight with a plate to ensure onions are totally immersed and leave for 12 hours.

Drain and peel onions and place in clean bowl. Mix remaining salt and water and pour over onions. Cover and leave for 24 hours.

Drain and wash onions. Pack into sterilised jars, leaving plenty of space at top.

Place vinegar, peppercorns, allspice, sugar, cloves and cinnamon stick in a saucepan. Stir over low heat till sugar dissolves. Bring to the boil, and simmer for 5 minutes.

Strain through a fine sieve and pour over onions until it comes at least 1 cm above them. Cover and leave for 3 months.

Makes 1 kg

TOMATO AND CUCUMBER PICKLE

3 kg green tomatoes, cored and sliced	**3** cloves garlic, finely chopped
3 cucumbers, peeled and thinly sliced	**1 litre** white vinegar
1 cup salt	**1½ cups** sugar
2 red capsicums (peppers), seeded and finely chopped	**1 tablespoon** mustard
	2 teaspoons turmeric
	1 teaspoon ground allspice
	1 teaspoon celery salt

Mix the tomatoes and cucumbers in a bowl, sprinkle evenly with salt and leave overnight.

The next day, wash and drain the tomato and cucumber mixture then combine with the remaining ingredients in a large saucepan. Cook gently for 1 hour, stirring occasionally, until the pickle reaches the desired consistency.

Pour into hot sterilised jars and seal. Store in a cool dark cupboard for up to 1 year. Refrigerate after opening.

QUICK APRICOT JAM

500 g dried apricots	juice and thinly pared rind
1.5 litres boiling water	**1** lemon
	1.5 kg sugar

Cut apricots into quarters and place in pressure cooker with water. Leave to soak for 1 hour.

Add lemon juice and rind and seal pressure cooker. Bring cooker to a medium, or 5 kg pressure and cook for 15 minutes. Slowly reduce pressure and remove cooker from heat. Discard pieces of lemon rind. Add sugar and stir until completely dissolved.

Return cooker to heat, without replacing lid, and bring jam to boiling point. Boil rapidly, stirring continuously, until setting point is reached or temperature on a sugar thermometer reaches 105°C (221°F). Cool jam slightly before bottling and sealing.

Makes 2.5 kg

PLUM JAM

2 kg blood plums	2 kg sugar
2½ cups water	

Chop plums into sections and remove stones. Place fruit and water in pan and simmer gently until plums are tender.

Meanwhile crack a few of the stones and remove kernels. Blanch them with boiling water and remove skins. Add kernels to fruit.

Remove pan from heat, add sugar and stir until completely dissolved. Return pan to heat and boil rapidly, stirring continuously and removing any scum that rises, until jam reaches setting point or temperature on sugar thermometer reaches 105°C (221°F).

Remove from heat and leave jam to cool for about 10 minutes before filling jars. Allow jam to cool thoroughly before sealing.

Makes about 3 kg

LEMON CURD

4 lemons	2 cups sugar
175 g butter	4 large eggs

Finely grate rind of 3 lemons. Cut lemons in half and extract juice, discarding pips.

Melt butter and sugar in a bowl set over a pan of hot water. Stir until smooth, without boiling.

Blend lemon rind and juice into mixture.

In another bowl, beat eggs. Pour them into lemon mixture, stirring constantly. Place over low heat and continue to stir, without boiling, for 30–40 minutes until mixture is thick and creamy.

Meanwhile, heat clean jam jars in a low oven. When curd is ready, pour into jars. Cover curd surface with waxed paper discs. Dampen top side only of cellophane discs and fix them on jars with rubber bands. Leave to cool — the curd will set to a soft jammy texture.

Store in a cool place and eat within a month.

Makes about 1 kg.

PATES

QUICK CHICKEN LIVER PATE
Pate de foie de volaille

125 g butter	200 g chicken livers, cleaned
1 small onion, finely chopped	1 sprig thyme
1 clove garlic, crushed (minced)	1 tablespoon brandy
	salt and pepper, to taste

Melt 25 g butter in a pan and gently fry the onions until tender, about 5 minutes. Add the garlic and cook a further 2 minutes.

Add liver and thyme to pan and cook, turning constantly for 5 minutes. Remove pan from heat and cool slightly. Place the mixture in a sieve and rub to form a smooth puree or process in a blender.

Add 75 g of the remaining butter and beat until smooth. Add brandy and seasoning to taste.

Spoon the pate into a serving dish or individual pate pots smoothing the top with a spatula. Melt remaining butter in a pan and pour over the pate. Refrigerate until set.

Serves 4

SMOKED TROUT PATE
Pate de truite fumee

3 medium-sized trout	½ teaspoon anchovy essence
60 g butter, softened	juice ½ lemon
3 slices white bread, crusts removed	salt and ground black pepper
¼ cup milk	
150 g cream cheese	

Remove head, skin and all bones from trout and puree flesh in a food processor or blender. Gradually add butter and blend well.

Soak bread in milk for 5 minutes, then squeeze out excess milk and add this and all remaining ingredients to pureed fish, blending constantly. Spoon mixture into well-oiled mould (approximately 2 cup capacity). Refrigerate overnight. Unmould pate and serve.

Serves 6–8

GIFTS FOR THE GOURMET

For those more discerning 'foodies' who really appreciate speciality food items, whether home-made or bought, a gourmet food parcel makes an excellent gift. (Also see page 28.)

David Jones

GIFTS FOR THE COOK

Every cook needs extra encouragement and inspiration from time to time — why not treat him or her to something special from the range of haute-cuisine kitchenware?

You can spend a fortune in an upmarket store, send costly flower deliveries by phone and shower your loved one with luxuries, but the gift that will always tug hardest at the heartstrings is the one you made yourself.

A simple linen handkerchief on which you've painstakingly embroidered their initial says far more about your kind heart and generosity than an impersonal set of shop-bought hankies. And you can buy a set of snazzy stationery anywhere, but how much more fun it is to receive a cleverly hand-decorated personal document holder in your favourite colours.

5 THE PERSONAL TOUCH

But while there's no limit to the range of beautiful handmade gifts the skilled crafts fan can devise, in this chapter we've concentrated on a huge selection of easy-to-make but effective tokens and gestures.

For instance, you need not be a champion knitter or seamstress to make our smashing 'landmark birthday' sweater or windcheater — a bit of dexterity with fabric pen, scissors and a needle and thread to stitch on motifs is the sum of the skill needed.

While making gifts usually offers the welcome opportunity to trim costs, it also implies far more thought, effort and concern than a present bought straight off the shop shelf.

As you don't need special skills for most of our handicraft ideas, many are ideal for children to make. Youngsters can easily put together egg warmers as Easter gifts, or make personalised paperweights for Fathers Day.

One of the most simple but successful do-it-yourself gifts is a voucher . . . for anything you choose. Spend a few minutes with paper, pens and scissors and you can make an impressive voucher exchangeable by Mum for one breakfast in bed when she wants, free washing up or a complimentary car wash for Dad when he's in need.

There is inspiration and guidance in this chapter for all age groups and many of our ideas can easily be adapted to suit your own schemes. Use them as a springboard and off you go!

Lois With Love   Mid City Granny May's Paper Shop

CHRISTMAS EMBROIDERY

Materials: white cross-stitch cloth (open weave) to size required; red, green and gold thread

To make: Follow pattern provided. This embroidery can be used as a card decoration or on a set of Christmas place cards; framed in a tiny gold frame, or simply presented as a gift in itself.

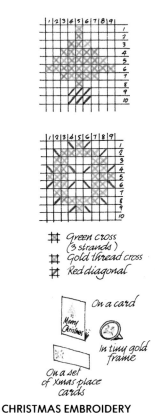

⊞ Green cross
  (3 strands)
⊞ Gold thread cross
⊞ Red diagonal

On a card

In tiny gold frame

On a set of Xmas place cards

CHRISTMAS EMBROIDERY

KISSING RING

Materials: wire coat hanger; florist's tape, bias binding or ribbon; florist's wire; greenery including holly; ribbon; mock berries or red bows

To make: Bend coat hanger into a ring and cover wire with florist's tape, bias binding or ribbon. Using florist's wire attach greenery around ring. Tie 3 pieces of ribbon (equal length) to ring and knot together on a curtain ring for hanging. Add mock berries or red bows to the arrangement for the finishing touch.
Note: A kissing ring has the same function as mistletoe but is more festive in spirit!

SANTA CLAUS FINGER PUPPET

Materials: felt (red, black, yellow, white); white pompon; red buttons; white lace; cotton wool

SANTA CLAUS FINGER PUPPET

White pompom
Felt
Lace
Felt
Buttons

CHRISTMAS FELT STOCKING

Materials: red, green and white felt; glitter pen and sequins (for variations)

Stocking: Make a simple template for stocking shape, pin onto green fabric or felt and cut out. Make print fabric band using top 7 cm of stocking template for correct shape and size. Applique stocking to front right side of sack. Right sides together sew side and bottom seams (1.5 cm width) leaving 1 cm gap in top hem at join for draw cord. Insert cord in top hem and knot ends together. Sew a small bell and bow onto centre of stocking band as the finishing touch.

KISSING RING

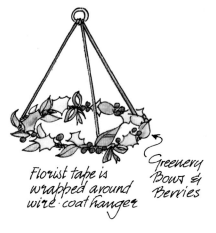

Florist tape is wrapped around wire coat hanger

Greenery Bows & Berries

CHRISTMAS GIFT SACK

Materials: red cotton fabric (88 cm × 62 cm); two 32 cm strips of ¼ in satin ribbon (white and green); green felt or cotton fabric for stocking (40 cm × 20 cm); print fabric for a 7 cm wide contrast band along top of stocking; red cord (1½ m)

To make: Fold longest side of fabric in half. Fold top edges over to wrong side and hem (2 cm width) — leaving 1 cm gap or more for draw cord to be inserted.

Position the two strips of satin ribbon across the top of front right side and sew into place.

CHRISTMAS FELT STOCKING

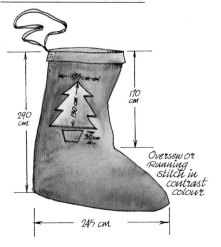

13.5 cm
19.0 cm
3.0 cm
290 cm
170 cm
245 cm

Oversew or Running stitch in contrast colour

CHRISTMAS GIFT SACK

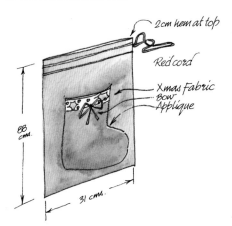

2cm hem at top
Red cord
Xmas fabric
Bow
Applique
88 cm
31 cms.

BEAR

Materials: felt; wadding; ¼ in ribbon ties; 2 in strip decorative braid; embroidery cotton or Slicker pens (for eyes and nose); ¼ in gold thread or gold ring for hanging

To make: Make a template of bear and cut out 2. Add ribbon tie and braid strip as shown. Embroider on eyes and nose or paint on using Slicker pens. Sew on gold thread loop or gold ring for hanging. Sew the 2 pieces together from top to toe, leaving inside leg area open. Stuff bear with wadding then finish sewing up.

Note: This bear makes a fun soft toy for baby's cot — also beautiful made up in dainty floral prints or a mixture of cheeky ginghams and bold colours. Machine sew and stuff carefully.

THREE BEARS MOBILE

For a set of three bears follow instructions for *Bear* — simply scale up for different sizes (Father bear and Mother bear). Tie bears onto rattan coat hanger or dowel. (Also see *Mobile*, (p. 63)

SOFT TOYS

Soft toys are very easy to make for gifts or decoration, usually involving a minimum of time, expense and materials. Materials normally used are felt and fun cotton fabrics (use up your collection of fabric scraps!); wadding for padding out toys, and odd bits and pieces like buttons, braid, ribbon, embroidery cotton and wool for details and finishing touches.

An almost endless range of simple shapes and characters can be made up from a very basic pattern. Our pattern for *Bear* is only one example and the steps for making it also apply for many other simple soft toys.

BOOT FOR BEAR

Materials: red felt or velvet; broderie anglaise lace and decorative braid (to match braid used for bear); gold trim (120 cm in length)

To make: Cut 2 red felt or velvet boot shapes to size given. Oversew edges leaving top open. Turn top hem down 1 cm. Tack broderie anglaise ruffle around top of boot then sew braid band over the top to finish. Sew gold

trim tie on inside boot. Place bear inside.

Note: This makes an excellent Christmas gift or decoration.

PILLOW CASE BEARS

Make 1 bear or 3 following instructions for *Bear*. Applique a 7 cm square fabric pocket onto a plain pillow case. Pop the small size bear inside pocket. (Make 3 pockets if 3 bears are used, leaving room for bear's head.)

TINY PILLOW BEAR

Make small size bear as above.

Pillow for Bear
Materials: calico; ¼ in ribbon for trim; wadding

To make: Cut out 3 pieces of calico, two 20 cm square pieces and one 8 cm square for pocket. Sew ribbon trim on pillow front, and then position pocket for bear in centre. Pin or tack right sides together with a 2 cm seam. Sew seams leaving one side unsewn. Turn pillow right side out and pad out with wadding. Sew up remaining side.

BEAR

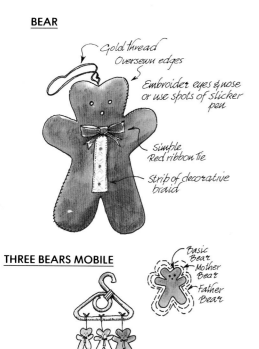

Gold thread
Oversewn edges
Embroider eyes & nose or use spots of slicker pen
Simple Red ribbon Tie
Strip of decorative braid

THREE BEARS MOBILE

Basic Bear
Mother Bear
Father Bear

BOOT FOR BEAR

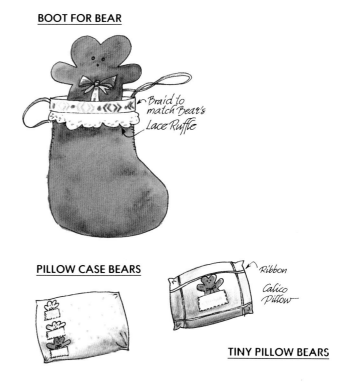

Braid to match Bear's
Lace Ruffle

PILLOW CASE BEARS

TINY PILLOW BEARS

Ribbon
Calico Pillow

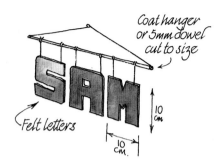

FELT NAME HANGING

Materials: felt, cotton wool or wadding; thread or ribbon ties; coat hanger or ¼ in dowel cut to size

To make: Make paper templates for letters of name (should be chunky, square style typeface) and cut out letters. Machine sew or oversew around edge by hand, stuffing with cotton wool or thin wadding as you go. Assemble as for *Mobile* (see p. 63)

FELT BADGE HOLDER

Materials: felt strip cut with pinking shears (85 cm × 8 cm); metal or wooden ring (7½ cm diameter); wide ribbon (80 cm × 4 cm) and thin ribbon (80 cm × 1 cm)
Note: Use the person's favourite colours, school colours, football colours.

To make: Turn top 5 cm of felt down over ring and sew fold in place. Sew first the wide ribbon down centre and then the thin ribbon down the centre of that. Turn in the bottom end of felt strip to form a point and sew to hold.

SIMPLE ADVENT CALENDAR

The above idea can also be adapted and used to make a simple Advent calendar. Use Christmas colours and thread two rows of wool through at regular intervals down felt strip to hold 24 sweets in position.

EASTER EGGWARMER

Materials: felt (different colours including yellow); sequins; Slicker pens

To make: Fold yellow felt over double and cut out 2 simple half egg shapes. Handstitch or oversew the 2 pieces together then decorate as preferred.
Suggestions: Cut out other simple felt shapes in contrasting colours e.g. eyes and beak or a Humpty Dumpty character, and sew or glue onto eggwarmer; sew on sequins; make pattern using Slicker pens.

FIVE FINGER PUPPETS

Rabbits for Easter

Materials: felt (different colours); 5 pompons for tails; small buttons; fabric or Slicker pens

FABRIC BAG

Materials: calico or another cotton fabric (86 cm × 36 cm); draw cord (1 m); felt for cut-out shapes

To make: Fold fabric in half. Fold top edges over 2 cm width to wrong side and hem. Sew side seams (1.5 cm width) leaving 1 cm gap in top hem at join for draw cord.

Insert draw cord and knot ends together. Decorate the bag by stitching on felt shapes or, alternatively, make a colourful pattern with fabric Texta or Slicker pens.
Note: This bag makes an excellent ham bag, holding a half leg of ham comfortably; scale up for full-sized ham.

EASTER EGG BASKET

Materials: cardboard (different colours); fabric scraps (e.g. cotton prints, lace) or wrapping papers (from sweets and chocolates); assorted ribbons

To make: Cut out cardboard to sizes given. Cut slits 2 cm wide to make flaps at points marked 'X'. Score the flaps and lines around square.

Glue flaps to box. Cut out a cardboard strip for handle and glue or staple in place. Decorate as preferred.

FELT BADGE HOLDER

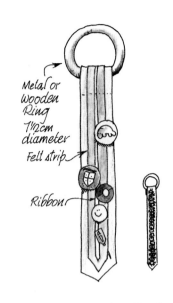

SIMPLE ADVENT CALENDAR

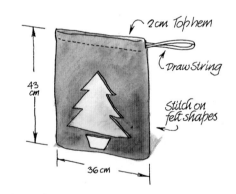

FABRIC BAG

EASTER EGG BASKET

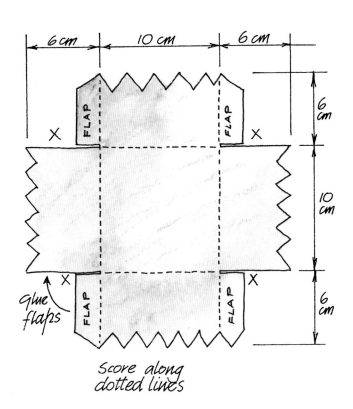

6 cm   10 cm   6 cm

FLAP   FLAP

6 cm

X   X

FLAP   FLAP

10 cm

X   X

6 cm

glue flaps

Score along dotted lines

EASTER EGGWARMER

8 cm

7½ cm

2 yellow felt shapes oversewn

Egg shape felt stuck on

Draw detail with slicker pen

Bird Clown

Glue pink to white ears

place ears between two basic shapes

Pin and sew by hand or machine

FIVE FINGER PUPPETS

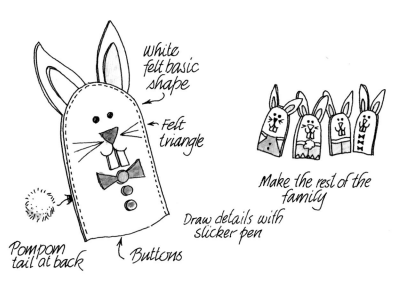

white felt basic shape

Felt triangle

Pompom tail at back

Buttons

Draw details with slicker pen

Make the rest of the family

SUPER QUICK GIFTS

BOOKWORM BOOKMARK

Materials: felt; cardboard; buttons for eyes

To make: Make a paper template for worm. Cut out worm shapes to size (about 150–200 mm in length) for both felt and cardboard. The cardboard shape should sit slightly inside the felt piece. Glue felt and board together. Sew on button eyes and add any other details like scales, stripes or dots with Slicker or fabric pens.

MOUSE BOOKMARK

Materials: felt (different colours); cotton thread for whiskers

To make: Make a paper template for mouse shape and cut out, using pinking shears for serrated edge. Cut out other pieces for eyes and mouse house and glue into place.

CHRISTMAS BOOKMARK

Materials: felt (Christmas colours); gold glitter pen or paint; Slicker pens

BOOKWORM BOOKMARK

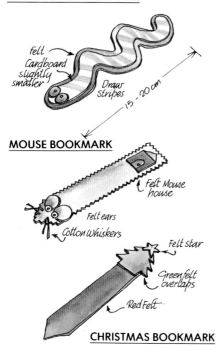

Felt
Cardboard slightly smaller
Draw stripes
15 - 20 cm

MOUSE BOOKMARK

Felt Mouse house
Felt ears
Cotton whiskers

Felt star
Green felt overlaps
Red felt

CHRISTMAS BOOKMARK

MEASURE-ME HEIGHT CHART

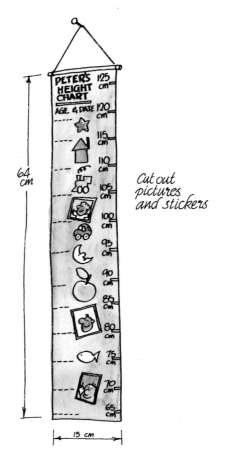

PETER'S HEIGHT CHART

AGE & DATE

125 cm
120 cm
115 cm
110 cm
105 cm
100 cm
95 cm
90 cm
85 cm
80 cm
75 cm
70 cm
65 cm

64 cm

Cut out pictures and stickers

15 cm

PAPER FLOWERS

Materials: coloured paper (e.g. soft pink, lemon, blue, red, violet); pipe cleaners for stems; Tippex; silver and gold paint; ribbon and bow

To make: Make paper templates of pieces (1), (2), (3) and (4). Cut out 7 or more flowers using templates as your cutting guide. Cut out the same number of centres in contrasting colours (3) and (4). Hole-punch each of the centres once. Put a skewer through the centre of flower pieces (1) then glue pieces (3) and (4) onto the appropriate flowers with holes matching up. Push a pipe cleaner through hole and bend tip to hold in place.

Flowers may be touched up and decorated with Tippex dots and gold and silver paint. To present, tie in a bunch with ribbon and a matching bow.

SUNNY FRIDGE MAGNETS

Materials: felt; cardboard; 8 cm square piece of stocking; wadding; magnetic tape (3 cm strip); beads for eyes

To make: Make a template for simple flower shape and circle to fit inside petals. Cut out shapes. Place small piece of wadding on circle, cover with stocking square and sew into place at back. Cut out other face details using contrasting colours, and sew or glue into place on flower circle. Sew on bead eyes. Glue circle/face to felt flower. Glue on magnetic strip at back.

DOCUMENT FOLDERS

Materials: cardboard folder and appropriate decoration — e.g. fabric motifs; cut-out pictures; ribbon; bows; paints; Texta; pens (gold, silver); Letraset; stickers; lace; picture or metal corners

MEASURE-ME HEIGHT CHART (ages 5 and under)

Materials: sheet of card (64 cm × 15 cm); cut-out pictures and stickers

To make: Use a ruler to mark heights in centimetres on the right side of card marking 65 cm at the base and going up to 125 cm. Use inch measurements on the other side (for those still thinking in Imperial measurement!).

Stick cut-out pictures and other visuals up the centre of the chart leaving several framed spaces for pictures of the growing child.

Write the child's name at the top of the chart.

GIRL'S HAIR COMBS AND BANGLES

Materials: a selection of plain hair combs and plastic bangles; Liberty bias binding and ribbons

PAPERWEIGHT

Materials: paperweight size, smooth rock or piece of wood (any shape); paint; polyurethane varnish

PAPER FLOWERS

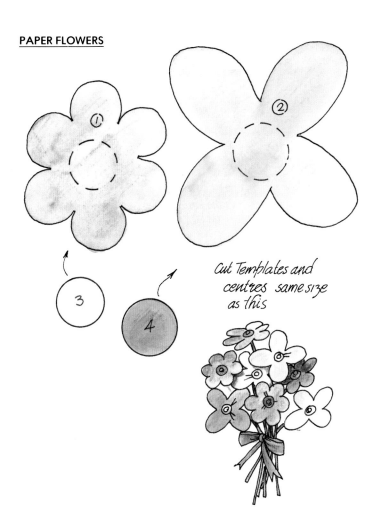

Cut Templates and centres same size as this

Smooth stone
Paint and finish with clear varnish.

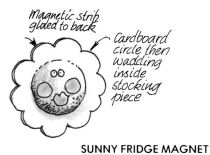

Magnetic strip glued to back

Cardboard circle then wadding inside stocking piece

SUNNY FRIDGE MAGNET

Place bias binding over top & catch with stitches. Turn in ends and sew in place

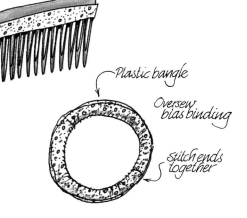

Plastic bangle

Oversew bias binding

Stitch ends together

DOCUMENT FOLDERS

For men
Felt pen stripes and dots

For women
fabric flower posy

Glued on ribbon trim

Tom the postman

For Children
Stamps and felt pen dots

HAIR COMBS AND BANGLES

61

PINATA (papier-mâché)

Materials: balloon; strips of newspaper; wallpaper paste; wrapped sweets, nuts and trinkets (no larger than 50 cent piece); 1 m nylon string; acrylic or powder paints and other decorations e.g. streamers, glitter, fabric strips, felt shapes

To make: Blow up a balloon and tie the end. Dip newspaper strips in paste and begin layering balloon. Cover balloon surface with two layers of paper strips, leaving a hole the size of a 50 cent piece at the wider end.

When these first two layers of paper are dry, prick the balloon (pull out pieces or leave in) and fill the pinata with the wrapped sweets, nuts and trinkets. Don't fill the pinata completely as it needs to hang from the ceiling and can't be too heavy.

Attach the string to the hole end of the pinata for hanging. Now place a further 2–3 layers of papier-mâché over the pinata covering the hole and tied end of string.

When the papier-mâché layers have dried completely, paint the pinata with bright colours to your own design, and add other decorations when the paint has dried.

Design ideas: animals (frogs, birds, fish, elephants); Humpty-Dumpties; Santa Claus (Christmas); bold abstract using primary colours.

WALL HANGING

Materials: hessian cloth (43 cm × 40 cm); ¼ in dowel (40 cm in length); ribbon; felt for cut-out shapes (different colours)

To make: Zigzag hem the two long sides and one short side of hessian. Turn down a 3 cm hem at the top and zigzag leaving a clear 2 cm space to slot dowel through. Make a slit in the ends of the dowel and knot the ribbon in slits for hanging.

Cut out the felt shapes you want, e.g. houses, clouds, animals — and arrange them on the hessian. Once you've worked out all relative positions of shapes either glue on or pin then sew on by hand using blanket stitch.

PINATA

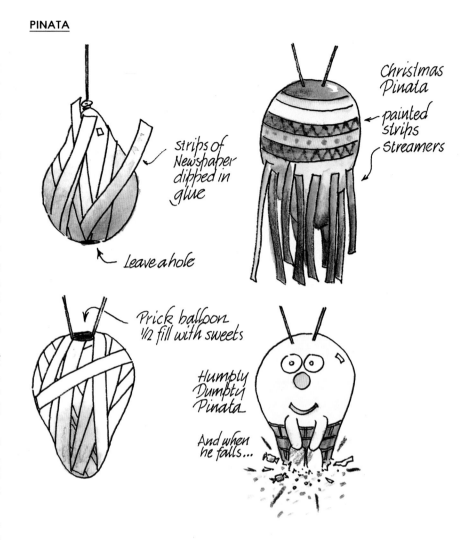

strips of Newspaper dipped in glue

Leave a hole

Christmas Pinata
— painted strips
— Streamers

Prick balloon ½ fill with sweets

Humpty Dumpty Pinata

And when he falls...

WALL HANGING

split dowel knot ribbon

Hem for dowel

Felt pieces stuck or appliquéd on to make a simple picture

Hem

POTPOURRI HANDKERCHIEF

Materials: appropriate handkerchief; potpourri mix (buy spicier mix for men); ribbon tie

POTPOURRI HANDKERCHIEF

HAT

Materials: plain straw hat; a selection of ribbons (narrow width); wide ribbon or cord for tie; slicker pens

To make: Using a wide-eyed needle, weave one ribbon along the edge of the hat leaving space for a second band of ribbon. Use Slicker pens for extra touches and add a lavish wide ribbon or cord tie for an elegant finish.
Note: If you want a very bold or dainty pattern, paint the rim with fabric paints.

HAT

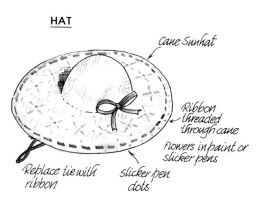

Cane Sunhat

Ribbon threaded through cane

Flowers in paint or slicker pens

Replace tie with ribbon

slicker pen dots

Paint rim with fabric paints in bold or dainty patterns

MOBILE

Materials: rattan or wire coat hanger (with ribbon wrapped around wire like tape to cover); 4 or more circles of bright coloured card (8.5 cm diameter); stickers or pictures to stick on circles; Slicker pens; ½ m of ¼ in ribbon

To make: Punch a hole in circles for ribbon. Decorate circles with stickers, pictures and Slicker pens. Thread ribbon ties through holes (cut to same or different lengths) and tie onto coat hanger.

ALTERNATIVES

Xmas Mobile: Make or buy 3 small Christmas toys or decorations for mobile.
Bear Mobile: Make 3 bears following instructions for *Three Bears Mobile* on page 57. Stick felt bears on card (front and back) as an alternative to padding out.
Note: Mobiles can be made out of many different materials and come in an incredible range of designs. Look at the commercial range for more ideas.

MOBILE

Cut out circles of card 8½ cm diameter Decorate with cut out pictures

VOUCHERS

Promises, promises! A voucher can cover a multitude of original gift ideas and are especially useful when faced with people who are very difficult gift-wise.

Whether your voucher is for car washing, breakfast in bed or dinner for two it can be beautifully presented as a gift in itself.

INITIALLING

Whether your gift item is a handkerchief, a set of table napkins, pillow cases or special notepaper, it can be made to look spectacular and personal at the same time with an embroidered or drawn initial.

Find a book on calligraphy at your local library, or buy one if the art of calligraphy really fascinates you. Copy out the initial letter or letters you want.

For cloth: Use tailor's chalk to draw letter design on cloth. Using needlework cotton satin stitch evenly over the outline. Chain stitch or another fancy stitch would also be appropriate.

Notepaper: Trace the letter design onto top left-hand corner or centre top of paper — try to choose a letter which incorporates leaves, branches and flowers in the design. Colour in with inks or coloured pencils. Notepaper can be scrolled and sashed with ribbon if that kind of presentation is right for the occasion.

CHILD'S FELT PURSE

Materials: felt (210 cm × 110 cm); large press stud; sequins; cut-out felt shapes and initials

To make: Fold over long side of felt up to 8 cm from top. Cut away 1 cm from each side of unfolded piece to form a flap. Stitch up two sides using running stitch. Sew on press studs to close purse. Decorate outside flap with sequins and cut-out shapes. Glue or sew on felt letters of the child's name below stud.

SPECIAL OCCASION LABELS

Materials: good quality bond paper; Letraset; gold, silver or coloured paint for decoration

MEMORY SWEATSHIRT OR WINDCHEATER

Materials: sweatshirt or windcheater; puff paints, fabric Texta or Slicker pens; sequins; buttons

To make: Cover sweatshirt or windcheater with drawings depicting important things in the person's life (hobbies, events, people). Depending on which landmark birthday or event it is, draw in 'X' number of meaningful symbols, e.g. 21 keys; 30 champagne glasses; 40 aeroplanes. Sew on sequins and buttons to accentuate your design. *Note:* To make this an even more memorable gift take the sweatshirt or windcheater along to the birthday party so that everyone can sign it.

PIRATE'S OUTFIT

Materials: black elastic; card; black paper; cardboard; silver foil; paints and Slicker pens.

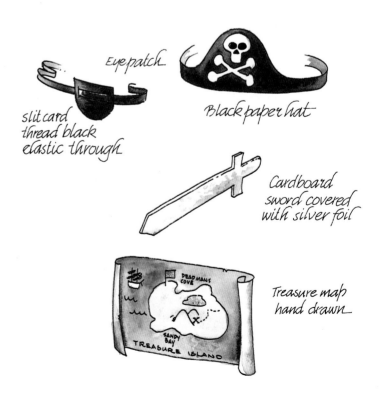

Eye patch

slit card thread black elastic through

Black paper hat

Cardboard sword covered with silver foil

Treasure map hand drawn

VOUCHERS

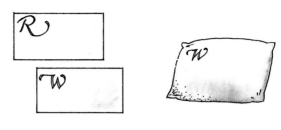
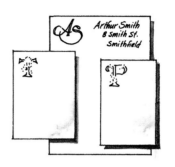

MEMORY SWEATSHIRT

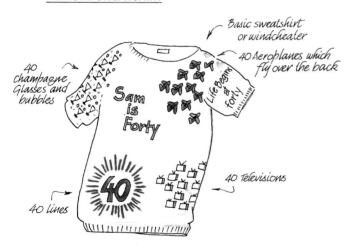

CHILD'S FELT PURSE

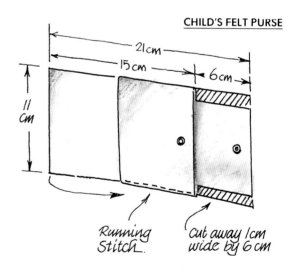

You're never too old to enjoy your birthday, even if you go to great lengths to conceal your age! However, each vintage presents its own problems to the gift giver so we've packed this chapter with guidance on the fads and fancies of each age group, together with ideas for celebrating those landmark birthdays.

Simple entertainment like finger puppets or mystery gift packages you've put together yourself often provide the biggest kick for the Under Fives, but once children are in school their tastes tend to become more informed and sophisticated.

6 MAKE A WISH!

Asking around will often uncover the latest craze among the five to 10-year-olds if you're looking for a trendy present but, as this age group is always game for fun activities, you can score as many points by putting together a more original gift like a surprise 'Fun Day-Out' voucher. Classic gifts for this age group are often items that proclaim a child's new level of 'maturity' — a watch indicating that they can now tell the time, or a simple camera that shows they're grown up enough to handle the responsibilities of a proper hobby.

For teenagers, a strong interest in pop music might dictate the classic gift of a guitar, while a swimming and surfing fan won't go wrong with a waterproof watch. Many teenagers love experimenting with fashion — clothes, shoes, make-up, jewellery, hairstyles — and a zany swag-bag packed with different eye shadows and pencils, lip gloss, face glitter, nail polish and skin care products or any fashion item of their choice, will be a very popular gift.

His or her tastes, hobbies and lifestyle are the best starting points when searching for that special gift — delight a clever cook with a starter kit for preparing her favourite new food fad; buy a selection of, say, Italian, Indian or Japanese food basics, any specialist equipment needed together with the appropriate cook book.

Mid City Granny May's Paper Shop

UNDER FIVE

Birthday gifts can be a hit or miss affair with the ruthlessly honest under fives. If a five-year-old likes your gift, it will be loved passionately! Other gifts may be ignored for a time, but revived with enormous success in twelve months time. The key is to buy thoughtfully, with some attention to the child's interests and abilities. The last minute chocolate frog you stick on top of your gift may get the greatest accolades!

Birthday Predictions
Monday's child is fair of face
Tuesday's child is full of grace
Wednesday's child is full of woe
Thursday's child has far to go
Friday's child is loving and giving
Saturday's child works hard for a
    living
But the child born on the Sabbath
    day
Is bonny and blithe and good and
    gay

CLASSICS

Pictorial china (for people without quarry tile kitchens), a special book (see booklists, pages 94–96), a rocking horse, a spinning top, engraved mug or spoon, an anthology of nursery rhymes or a silver bangle, clothes, shoes.

THE PERSONAL TOUCH

The secret of success with gift packages for this age group lies in presentation. ALWAYS put their name somewhere on the package, and match your collection to their age and interests. You don't need to buy all the items mentioned for each kit — three or four may be enough.

Finally, be prepared to spend a little time sharing their enjoyment. (Cut and paste can be quite therapeutic for adults!)

✳ Do-It-Yourself Finger Puppets — Sew five basic shapes in different coloured felt (for example: rabbit, cat, elephant, parrot, mouse), and present in a special box with buttons, feathers, cut-out pieces of felt (in the shape of eyes, mouths etc) for them to add on the appropriate faces, hair, and personality to each character. (See *Finger Puppets*, p. 59).

✳ Cut, Paste and Paint Kit — Paints, brushes, paper, wallpaper, paste, pasta, stickers, stamps, pipe cleaners, pictures from magazines and cards, crepe paper and an apron, all arranged in a labelled paper folder, or a covered shoe box, will give hours of fun.

✳ Colourful Wall Hanging — Wall hangings are a delightful way to decorate wall space for a nursery or child's bedroom. You can make up your own picture design and colour scheme to suit. See *Wall Hanging* on page 62.

✳ Set of Play Blocks — A set of simple timber offcuts make excellent play blocks for toddlers. Paint or stain them using bright coloured acrylic paints or polyurethane for a clear finish.

✳ Pinata — Pinatas are decorative clay or papier-mâché pots filled with sweets and treats and suspended from the ceiling. To get at the sweets inside the children beat the pinatas with sticks until they break open. The custom of making pinatas originates from Mexico. A papier-mâché pinata is easy to make and is an attractive decoration. The tradition of breaking a pinata open with a stick may be a little over the top, in which case, try cutting it open! (See *Pinata* making instructions, p. 62.)

✳ P.S. More Ideas — Soft toys; mobiles; books; musical/sound toys; play equipment; nursery rhyme and story cassette tapes; Bunnikins plate and mug; Lego.

✳ Sandpit Gear — Buckets, spades, balls (this basic equipment is very versatile and can be used in dirt, a sandpit, or on the beach).

✳ Travel Box/Rainy Day Box/Sick Child's Box — Crayons, coloured gummed paper, compass, road maps, glue, buttons, cards, balloons, magnifying glass, scissors, games and puzzles.

✳ Postman Pete's Parcel/Tom the Postman — Decorate an envelope folder with stamps, stickers, and the child's own address. On the inside cover stick a small secret envelope containing twenty 1 cent stamps and twenty 2 cent stamps. Add airmail stickers, telegram forms, post office information forms, envelopes, brown paper and string, a packet of labels, scissors, and notebook.

✳ Teddy Bear's Picnic Package — Most children will have a teddy or another toy who is always ready for a picnic. To make your package, arrange a check napkin for a tablecloth, small plastic cups and plates (or a tea set), extra teddy bears, and teddy bear biscuits and cakes in a small cane basket.

✳ Quick and Easy Fancy Dress Costumes — Children love dressing up and disguising themselves as exciting fantasy figures. With a little sewing and a few extra bits and pieces you can create a fantasy wardrobe full of fun characters.

Pirate — eye patch, treasure map, bandana, sash, treasure, striped shirt or T-shirt, play sword, cash box full of gold coins (chocolate), stuffed parrot (to sit on shoulder). For more ideas see *Pirate Outfit* on page 64.

Nurse or Doctor — bandages, tiny bottles of pills (small sweets) and medicines (coloured water), plastic spoons, first aid box with red cross painted on it, a play stethoscope, a white coat (doctor), a white head cap (nurse).

Cowboy — cowboy hat, cardboard star covered with foil for law badge, bandana, toy gun with holster, lasso, boots, jeans.

King or Queen — cardboard crown, cloak, wand or sceptre, crown jewels, throne.

Fairy — silver crown, cloak (with cardboard and felt wings sewn on), wand, bells on a pair of dancing slippers, jar of magic dust (glitter), a book of magic.

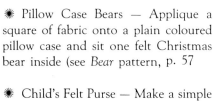

✳ Pillow Case Bears — Applique a square of fabric onto a plain coloured pillow case and sit one felt Christmas bear inside (see *Bear* pattern, p. 57

✳ Child's Felt Purse — Make a simple felt purse and add your own special design and colour touches (see *Felt Purse*, p. 64).

✳ Activity Bag — Decorate a drawstring bag (see *Fabric Bag*, p. 58) with puff paint, fabric pens, applique or felt collage. Use strong fabric for wear and tear of stationery and drawing equipment.

✳ Giant Biscuit — Use a gingerbread biscuit mix (see recipe, p. 49) and make into one large shape e.g. a giant, flower, tree, face. After baking, decorate the biscuit with icing, smarties and a small toy. Make a hole with a skewer and thread on a small gift card.

BIRTHDAY PARTY!

Arrange a special birthday party for your child with all the trimmings — delicious food, fun games, balloons, streamers, a fabulous cake.

CHILDREN'S PARTY CHECKLIST

✳ Choose a location, theme and time, the more original, the better.

✳ Send out interesting invitations two to three weeks ahead; try to keep the guest list small.

✳ Choose the menu and do as much as possible ahead of time. (Check now if any guests have special dietary needs.)

✳ Prepare house for the intended horde — clear away all valuables and establish 'off limits' boundaries such as bedrooms, studies, etc.

✳ Ensure that all children can be delivered and picked up at the nominated times; have a list of contact numbers for parents in case of emergency or illness.

✳ Ask another adult to help out and give you support for the afternoon. You'll need it!

✳ Decorate party area with balloons, streamers and posters, anything that's bright and cheery.

✳ Give the children plenty of room to move and make a mess; preferably outdoors.

✳ Have on hand a good supply of prizes, at least one for every child. Extras may come in handy in case of tantrums!

✳ Be sure your home and yard are safe for party activities; inform your neighbours of the event so they can keep a lookout for 'escapees' and wanderers!

✳ Keep pets away from the party zone; they may frighten timid guests or tempt little terrors!

✳ Arrange a set of rainy-weather alternative games and activities.

✳ Assemble goodie bags as far ahead of time as possible; make a few spares for last-minute arrivals and some for brothers and sisters.

Apple Bobbing: Best as an outdoor activity, fill large tubs or buckets with water, place whole or halved apples in the water and challenge children to retrieve the apples using teeth only. Sure to cause splashes but lots of fun!

Musical Statues: A variation on the musical chairs theme, each guest must dance and move about while the music is played; when it stops suddenly, each must freeze perfectly still. Those who fail to do so are eliminated until there's a final winner.

Treasure Hunt: With secret little treasures hidden throughout the house and garden, issue each guest a clue that leads them to the next clue, and the next, until eventually they uncover the booty. Small amounts of coin money are always well-received.

Eat The Chocolate: Watch how fast children consume the prize in this game! You'll need a hat, gloves, sunglasses, scarf and a pair of large boots plus a jumbo-sized block of chocolate, knife, fork and plate. Place the above in the middle of a circle of children and give them a couple of dice. Each child takes turns at rolling the dice until someone lands on a six; they then leap into the middle of the circle, don all the apparel then begin to eat the chocolate using the knife and fork. Meanwhile, the other players continue to roll the dice until another six is thrown. The winner then assumes the chocolate-eating role, even if the previous winner has only just managed to fit the gloves! It's frenzied fun in a mad race for just one bite of the chocolate!

SCHOOL AGE CHILDREN

The school age child has more definite ideas about what he or she would like for a birthday gift. You can ask them directly or go it alone with a creative gift of your own devising.

At this age most children have well-developed hobbies and interests which they enjoy, whether it's collecting marbles or skateboarding. There is bound to be something they want very much!

CLASSICS

For a school age child, a first watch, bike, charm bracelet, cricket bat (or any other sports equipment), leather wallet, chess set, writing set, camera, or encyclopaedia are all classic gifts.

THE PERSONAL TOUCH

A parcel of gifts for a school age child should be as interesting and creative as possible. Here are some simple ideas for pleasing parcels.

✳ Going to School Kit — It's their biggest event so far, so acknowledge it with a useful collection of things they'll need like a lunch box, drink flask, ruler, name stickers, library bag, and a pencil case full of pencils, Texta pens and rubbers.

✳ Super-Quick Gifts — Felt badge holder, Bookworm or Mouse bookmark, fridge magnet, decorated combs and bangles (see page 60).

✳ Birthday Treat Voucher — Decorate a card as a voucher with appropriate art work. The 'treat' may be a train ride; a visit to the zoo, a museum, a pantomime, a movie, the beach. Make them a friend of the zoo or a National Trust member to mark your visit to either the zoo or a museum.

✳ Bike Rider's Kit — A terrific gift to go with that first two-wheeler when excitement is at fever pitch. Fill a drawstring bag or paper folder with a personalised cloth cap, complete with cyclist's motif sewn on, leaflets, stickers, pump and maps.

✳ Learn to . . . Kit — For example, learn to knit. Wind some tiny balls of wool (including a good range of colours); add some small needles and place in a draw-string bag with a voucher promising 5–10 Easy Lessons.

✳ Odds and Ends Package — Many children will love this odd-ball assortment of a compass, false teeth, magic tricks, stickers, pens, octopus hooks, magnifying glass, suction toy, tennis balls and a deck of cards.

✳ Football or Cricket Match Kit — All you need is a beanie hat, badges, cards, laces, rosettes, small sachets of tomato sauce (for the pie), posters and a voucher promising to take them to a match! It's a winner.

✳ Birthday Tree — For any age, a delightful birthday tradition is to plant a tree which can grow with the child.

✳ Computer Whizzkid Pack — Put together a set of challenging new computer games.

✳ P.S. More Ideas — Games (Dungeons and Dragons, dominoes, Lego etc); hobby kits (stamp-collecting, photography etc); personalised items (books, bags, wallets, diaries, sports gear).

David Jones
Mid City Granny May's Paper Shop

TEENS

It's often hard to find the right gift for a person whose age, lifestyle and interests are different from your own. This is particularly true with teenagers.

There are three ways to cope:
- ☐ **Put yourself in their shoes, find out their interests and passions and *listen* to them.**
- ☐ **Buy 'safe' classic gifts which they may not be wild about now, but will enjoy later (e.g. a modern classic book).**
- ☐ **Give them money — it never fails to please. If giving hard cash worries you, buy gift vouchers (books, records, tapes, CDs) or open a bank or building society account in their name.**

CLASSICS

For teenagers, the classics overlap with the selection and price range of adult classics — leather, silk, music, literature, reference books, dated plates, silver and gold, watches and pens, quality accessories, games like Scrabble, Monopoly, Backgammon or Mahjong, are all reliable gifts. Clothes, and especially the latest gear, is also very high on the list.

The right classic gift depends on the talents and interests the teenager has. If he or she is musical, it may be a guitar; for a swimmer, an underwater watch; for a budding writer, a gold pen and so on. Keep your credit card handy!

THE PERSONAL TOUCH

✳ Crazy Makeup Swag — Bundle up a zany collection of eye makeup, lipsticks, face glitter, hairspray, nail polish, and a jar of cold cream, in a bright scarf. Or fill a case or bag with creams, tonics, masks and moisturisers.

✳ Favourite Foods — Discover their weaknesses and indulge them (e.g. chocolate, favourite biscuits, popcorn, marshmallows, etc). See Chapter 4 for more ideas.

✳ Study Special — Make up a zany stationery parcel of pencils, pens, rubbers, magnets, folders, spring clips, paper clips, scribblers, stapler, dictionary, calculator and pencil sharpener.

✳ Surfing Survival Kit — T-shirt, board shorts, lip balm, tanning lotions, zinc cream, sun visor, sun shades, wine cask pillow, windbreaker.

✳ Hair Care Parcel — Wrap up a selection of hair products: conditioner, shampoo, combs, brush, ribbons, hair bands and clips.

✳ Sneakers Supreme — A pair of white sneakers with fabric Texta for a do-it-yourself design.

✳ T-Shirt Design Kit — Set of fabric paints and brushes with some information on how to go about it.

✳ Voucher — A voucher can be a low risk, fun alternative to buying a very individual gift, e.g. record or tape voucher, book voucher or a home-made voucher for the movies, the theatre or a ticket to the rock concert of their choice.

✳ All-Purpose Voucher — Not quite as bad as an open cheque! Give them a choice; this could entail a shopping trip to buy some new clothes; a course of lessons e.g. guitar, typing; a special meal out for him or her plus a friend; a weekend trip away. Perhaps you could offer your own expertise or time as a gift in the form of five lessons e.g. sailing, tennis, golf, woodwork, cooking, sewing, driving.

✳ Needlework Kit — If you think your child will enjoy one of the more genteel arts, needlework can be an absorbing, creative hobby. For a beginner: cottons, needles, fabric, hoops and a book or manual on needlework which features simple projects for the novice.

HER BIRTHDAY

Whether she is your wife, daughter, mother, niece, girlfriend or grandmother Her birthday matters! It's the perfect opportunity to wow her with a fabulous gift presented in a flurry of ribbons, bows and wraps.

CLASSICS

Birthstones
January — Garnets
February — Amethysts
March — Bloodstones/Aquamarines
April — Diamonds/Rock Crystal
May — Emeralds
June — Agates/Moonstone, Pearl
July — Rubies/Cornelian
August — Sardonyx/Peridot
September — Sapphires/Lapis lazuli
October — Opals
November — Topaz/Golden Quartz
December — Turquoises

Because so many classics for women involve very personal, feminine items it is often wise to involve her in the decision-making; unless you know exactly what she wants — right down to perfect fit. Gold, silver, leather, silk, cotton, wool and cashmere go to make up the classic line of gifts for her wardrobe.

A shopping trip is one safe option and can include a delicious morning tea, lunch or afternoon tea along the way. If that's not possible find out what she wants and ensure that the gift can be returned and exchanged if it's unsuitable.

THE PERSONAL TOUCH

✴ Pamper Hamper — She may be a busy mum or a hectic career woman; either way this collection could be a lifesaver: music (record or tape); chocolates; a book or glossy magazine; her favourite perfume or bubble bath; a breakfast in bed or candle-lit dinner for two voucher, and a glorious bunch of flowers.

✴ Birthday Cake — Order a specially designed cake to be delivered.

✴ Promises, Promises — Spoil someone you care about with a voucher promising something they want or need: new hair cut; a massage; a beauty treatment; a manicure or a weekend at a health farm; a gym subscription; a voucher for picture framing, curtain making, a floristry course; babysitting or a free choice of plants from a favourite nursery. If you're looking for the unusual, write a voucher promising a little black dress of her choice, tailor made or off the peg.

✴ Green Fingers — If she adores working outside in the garden it's simply a matter of finding out what she needs. It may be a bright new rubbish bin or wheelbarrow, a new broom, rake, edger, plant food, watering can, gloves.

A gardening book or diary is also a great gift especially if she already has lots of gardening equipment. Also see Chapter 3 for more ideas.

✴ Specialist Gift Wrapping Box or Basket — This is a terrific gift in itself, and very useful particularly if she likes to put lots of thought and flourish into gifts for other people. Fill a box or cane, basket with all the essential materials: selection of wrapping papers (colour coordinated, novelty, tissue papers, cellophane etc); ribbons; tape; stickers; cards; scissors. Make sure you present it to her exquisitely wrapped! Your package might also include a book on the finer arts of gift wrapping.

✴ Haute Cuisine — What sort of food and cooking does she love? Italian? French? Spanish? Japanese? Buy a selection of prepared foods from the chosen country, any specialist equipment if it's required, and a cook book. Vive la différence!

✴ Alfresco Parcel — This is the ideal gift if she is an outdoors person who loves picnics. Parcel up in a hamper or basket: a red gingham cloth, napkins, chunky cutlery and glasses plus some exotic edibles like pates, cheeses and fruits.

HIS BIRTHDAY

Here is your chance to make HIS birthday something really special! Does he really need more socks and hankies?

Too often we limit our options to the conservative when buying or making gifts for men. It doesn't have to be that way especially if he is an active person with lots of interests and an imagination just waiting to be captured!

The right gift defies age and gender, and focuses in some quintessential way on him, his qualities, needs and aspirations. With a little research it's easy to find out about his secret passions, favourite colours, and how best to reach his heart through his stomach!

CLASSICS

Refresh your memory with a look at some of the Fathers Day classics (p. 27) and Lifestyle and Special Interest gifts (p. 92). Classic gifts for men, like women, are often in the category of jewellery, clothes, toiletries and accessories, e.g. a gold watch, a silver tie pin, cuff links, silk shirt, sweater; or hobby and sports oriented, e.g. accessories for golf, fishing, driving, winter sports and so on.

THE PERSONAL TOUCH

✳ Lazy Lounger — If he's generally a very busy man, by nature or by profession, why not encourage him to relax? Give him a deck chair or a hammock, a sun hat, a good book or magazine and a supply of his favourite food, savoury or sweet.

✳ Connoisseur's Platter — His expertise may be wine, chocolate or cheese; as a connoisseur he will appreciate your efforts. If his special area is cheese make up a variety of cheeses on a platter (Stilton, Port Salut, Brie, Tasty, Edam) and present it to him with a Swedish cheese knife, a selection of watercrackers and olives, garnished with a bunch of fresh white grapes. If you really want to spoil him throw in an excellent bottle of claret for good measure!

✳ Toiletries — Restock his supply of a favourite brand, or make up a selection including soap, deodorant, eau de cologne, shampoo, novelty toothbrush, aftershave lotion.

✳ Book Collector — Find out what kinds of books he likes and collects. He may collect rare eighteenth or nineteenth century first editions; or specific genres of twentieth century fiction (detective; pulp; thrillers; horror; popular romance; western). If you enjoy haunting second-hand bookshops it will be a pleasure seeking out a book which your collector will cherish. If he enjoys vintage crime writers you'll be looking for names like Agatha Christie, Dashiell Hammett, Conan Doyle, Georges Simenon, Raymond Chandler, G. K. Chesterton, E. D. Biggers.

✳ Voucher — Promises, promises! Let him rest while you do odd jobs for him; it might be weeding the garden, lawnmowing, mending, painting or housework. If he's more sophisticated in his tastes you could offer him a night out, including movies or theatre and dinner; an art exhibition or visit to a museum followed by lunch; a professional massage or sauna.

✳ Sweet Tooth — If he finds sweet things irresistible, why not make him a happy man? Make up an assortment depending on what he likes, e.g. humbugs, chocolate frogs and jellybeans! If he's a licorice nut: straps, licorice allsorts, cigarettes, bullets, chocolate covered; presented in glossy black wrapping paper with bright, multicoloured ribbon trimmings.

✳ P.S. More Ideas — Underwear (sexy or sensible!), tie, bow tie, stationery, chair, floppy discs, compact disc (CD), cassette tape, lottery tickets, record, binoculars, sports gear, shirt, decanter.

THE BIG ONES

COUNTDOWN — 18, 21 . . .

The 'big' birthdays are important events for us all, and often mark the beginning of new phases and experiences in our lives.

Eighteen and twenty-one are special birthdays which celebrate a coming of age. Traditionally the 'coming out' age was twenty-one, and the birthday girl or boy was given a key as the symbol of their official entry into society and the world of adults.

Nowadays, when a young person turns eighteen they are legally entitled to vote, drink and drive; and so this birthday has assumed more significance, even though twenty-one is still widely celebrated as an important birthday.

CLASSICS

Gifts of china, glassware, watches, jewellery, literature, gold pens, silver collectable antiques and tailored clothes all make lasting gifts.

THE PERSONAL TOUCH

To make a successful gift package, carefully consider the current interests of the young person you are buying for. Your package might result in a specialist car care kit, a sports kit, a 'leaving home' kit, a handyperson's kit, a chocolate lover's kit, or a surfer's kit.

✳ Pass on a special book, an antique piece of jewellery, or a family heirloom that you have loved and feel ready to hand on to the next generation.

✳ Newsclipping Photo Book — This is a plan ahead gift, but worth the effort. Decide now to start collecting newspaper cuttings and photos in a folder, ready to put together for an eighteenth or twenty-first birthday presentation.

✳ Buy a loose-leaf photo album and a supply of pens. Take a polaroid camera to the party, and photograph everyone present. Mount the picture on a page, on the spot, and ask each person to write a few words underneath. This is a great action memento and a gift well worth the over-time involved.

COUNTDOWN — 30, 40, 50, 60 . . .

The countdown has begun but there's absolutely no need for anyone to go into a decline! By now people have a fairly good idea of who they are, what they want and how to go about it — and this will be reflected in their tastes and lifestyle.

Thirty signals a goodbye to our twenties and hello to the prime of our lives. For most of us it's a time of great personal growth and reassessment often resulting in a change of lifestyle or career.

While forty falls fair and square into middle age it's by no means 'old'. Currently, in fact, forty is a rather fashionable, fun age to be! It can be quite settled or in a complete state of topsy-turvy not unlike life at twenty or thirty!

Fifty and sixty can also be times of enormous change and rediscovery. In many ways this age group has far more time to indulge in exciting new interests and activities.

CLASSICS

They may already have many of the 'classic' items, so you'll need to give some thought to a gift which they can add to their existing collection of china, silver, glass, jewellery, music, literature and so on.

You may want to give them a more frivolous gift, if so, put together a package which focuses on their eccentricities in some way e.g. their love of soaps (give them the ultimate soap-lover's collection, each soap beautifully wrapped).

Look particularly at their lifestyle and special interests for more ideas (see lists on pages 92–93).

THE PERSONAL TOUCH

What are the person's priorities in life? Are they married, single or undecided? In a new home, or renovating an old one? A nostalgic '60s buff, or an '80s yuppie? A born again gardener or opera fan? Whatever the person's age and interests are, inspire them with your gift.

✳ Buy some bottles of champagne and relabel them with celebration labels. It's fun reminiscing about the occasion each time a bottle is opened.

✳ A hand-knitted sweater, a bed quilt or wall hanging all make super gifts if you have the time or expertise. If you don't, commission someone else who does, to make it for you.

✳ Memory Sweatshirt or Windcheater — Same idea as an autograph book — buy a plain sweatshirt or windcheater, bring along some fabric pens and get everyone to sign it or decorate it in some way. Present it to the birthday person at the end of the evening as a fun gift. Also see page 64.

✳ Timber! — Buy a special gift made of wood (modern or antique, practical or purely decorative, large or small). Add a small, discreet brass or silver plaque engraved with the person's name and the date.

✳ Autograph Book — Sounds corny but can be quite a treasure in retrospect. Ask everyone present at the celebration to write something inside.

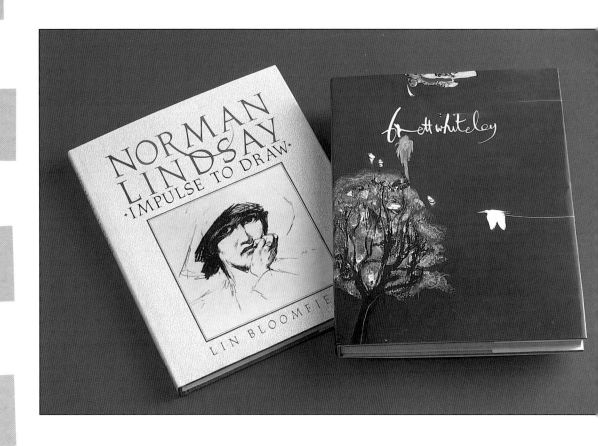

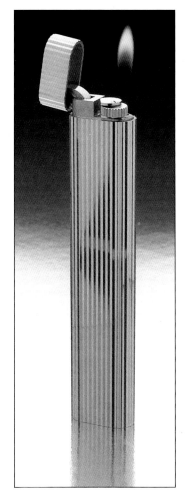

Family events and milestones like weddings, births, anniversaries and retirement are an important part of life's tapestry, so we've devoted this chapter to devising gifts and commemorations for these and other landmark occasions that will delight donor and recipient alike, lingering in everyone's memory for years to come.

The predictability of such events needn't limit our choice of gift to the traditional — unless you're restricted to a wedding list, for instance, engagements and marriages offer plenty of opportunity for imaginative gifts.

7 A TIME TO CELEBRATE

If you know only one half of a betrothed couple, cut out the question of taste by putting together a practical package of barbecue equipment, a kitchen cleaning kit or a rather more festive cocktail kit.

The arrival and christening of a new baby inevitably heralds a shower of presents but, if you don't want to run with the pack and give clothing, toys or nursery equipment, consider some original ideas which can be expanded into lifelong and valuable keepsakes — a silver charm for a bracelet which can be added to year after year, or a case of wine to be laid down and opened on the child's 21st or wedding day! If you can afford to honour your loved ones with silver, gold or precious stones, the choice of gift on milestone occasions like anniversaries and retirements is simple, but most of us have to put in a bit of effort and come up with rather more original ideas — theatre tickets, a voucher for a meal in a special restaurant or even the gift of a photographic portrait to commemorate the event. Why not launch someone into retirement by sending them off on their first hot air balloon ride, or helicopter trip? At least they can't complain that retirement is dull!

Moving house is an upheaval in anyone's life, so you'll provide a welcome light in the darkness of all those packing cases if you turn up on the new doorstep with a bottle of champagne, or a thoroughly practical package of necessities like rubber gloves, lightbulbs, scissors and any other vitals likely to have got lost in the move!

David Jones   Hampshire and Lowndes   Lois With Love   Mid City House and Garden   Mid City Granny May's Paper Shop

ENGAGEMENTS AND WEDDINGS

For both engagements and weddings, the fun and frustration often lies in having to buy for a couple instead of a single person. You may know one half of the combination very well, but not the other half. Nevertheless, they're about to become a team, and your gift needs to reflect that.

A peek into *Emily Post* or *Bride's Magazine* will give you a sense of the rich tradition of weddings and betrothals: publishing the banns, flowers for the church, appropriate outfits, correct gifts for the attendants, the engagement and wedding speeches.

But for better or worse, wedding ceremonies today take many forms, from the registry office to an outdoor wedding to formal church weddings.

Engagement and wedding gifts too have changed. Often there's less economic need for a Hope Chest or Glory Box, as couples may have much of the household equipment needed well before they're formally married.

The key note with gifts is flexibility. But what they need and want, not what tradition says is appropriate.

CLASSICS

Gifts of glass, silver, linen and china are the recognised traditional wedding gifts. And because we usually spend larger amounts of money on these items, careful research is needed.

There are two basic types of classic gifts. There are the useful utilitarian classics like everyday china, dinner plates, cake plates, or the special occasion classics like a silver gravy boat, candelabra, or a salt cellar. Choose whichever you feel comfortable with. Both types of gifts will last for years, but one gives daily pleasure, the other comes out only for best.

For an unusual engagement gift, give a beautiful chest as a mock Hope Chest. In colonial USA every girl had one of these to hold her handcrafted pieces ready for married life. A beautiful chest like this has many functions — storage, decorative, a seat, a table, perhaps even a toy box.

The classic gift to the bride from the groom is jewellery, and for the groom from the bride, a gold pen, clock, briefcase, watch or luggage.

THE PERSONAL TOUCH

Practical packages make excellent engagement and wedding gifts, for example, an alfresco kit (barbecue equipment; picnic hamper with all necessary items included), gardener's kit, pasta lover's kit, or cocktail kit.

Make up a starter kit of useful household items for the kitchen, laundry or garage. Include gadgets and tools and intersperse with commercial products.

✻ House Plant — Give a plant with an appropriate folk lore association (white chrysanthemums stand for truth, lilies for purity, violets for faithfulness, and orange blossom for fertility).

✻ Start a collection of items you can add to over the years — silver, china, vintage port, paperweights, books.

✻ Engrave a date and names or initials discreetly on spoons, or a silver tray.

✻ Monogrammed towels, pillowcases, linen may seem old-fashioned, but they look special, they last, and will always be remembered.

✻ Videotape the wedding and the reception. Tape record the wedding speeches. They're often the best part and soon forgotten.

✻ Commission a unique, one-off wedding gift — a piece of pottery, glass, an artwork, tapestry, stained glass, or a piece of jewellery.

✻ Is there a useful service you could offer a couple starting life together? Perhaps curtain making, garden watering over the honeymoon period, fence painting, or a day's hard labour on their new home would be appreciated.

Note: It's an excellent idea to combine forces and buy a very expensive gift in a group, e.g. dishwasher, washing machine, dryer etc.

Hampshire and Lowndes Mid City House and Garden
Lois With Love   Mid City Granny May's Paper Shop
Made Where

PS MORE IDEAS

Lots of stores have a bridal register, with lists like the one below. You might like to make up your own list of expensive and not so expensive gifts for friends to choose from.

For the Kitchen
apron
bottle opener
mixing bowls
bun tins
breadboard and knife
cake tins
can opener
capuccino maker
casserole dish
cheese grater
china dinner service
chocolate making
    equipment
coffee grinder
coffee percolator
coffee mugs
colander
copper bowls
cookery books
double boiler
egg cups
egg coddlers
fire extinguisher
flan tins
fondue set
food processor
fruit bowls
garlic press
graters
jam pot
juicer
kettle
liquidiser
lemon squeezer
measuring jugs and cups
microwave oven
mincer
cake mixer
blender
nutcracker
omelette pan
oven-proof dishes
oven gloves
pasta maker
pastry board
peelers
pestle and mortar
pedal bin
pressure cooker
pudding basins
roasting pan
salt and pepper shakers
    or mills
sandwich maker
salad bowls
saucepans

scales
scissors
steel or nylon sieves
skillet
souffle dishes
spatulas
spice containers
storage jars
sugar bowl
tea pot
tea towels
terrarium
thermometers
thermos
toaster
toast rack
trays
vegetable steamers
vertical grill
whisks
wine cooler
wok and utensils
wooden spoons

For the Bathroom
bath mat
towels
bathroom scales
hairdryer
hand towels
shower accessories
towel rack

For Formal Dining
butter dish
cake plate
candles
candlesticks
candelabra
carafe
carving dish
cheese knife
cheese platter
coasters
corkscrew
coffee set
cruet set
dessert dishes
gravy boat
hostess trolley
icebucket
icehammer
napkins
placemats
placecard holders
serving dishes
serviette rings

silver tray
soup tureen
tablecloth
tablepiece
wine
wine labels
wine rack

For the Bedroom
alarm clock
bedside table
bedspread
blankets
chest of drawers
continental quilt
electric blanket
hatstand
lamps
pillows and pillow cases
quilt covers
sheets (single and double)
valances
waste paper baskets
wardrobe

Cutlery
cake knives and forks
cake server
fish knives and forks
grapefruit knives
kitchen knives
serving utensils
steak knives
teaspoons

Glassware
brandy balloons
champagne flutes
claret glasses
cocktail glasses
cocktail shaker
decanter
dessert bowls and dishes
water jug
whisky glasses
wine glasses

For the Garden/
Outdoors
bird feeder
bird bath
barbecue
compost bin
decorative pots
electric drill
garden tools
garden gnome
hammock

lawnmower
outdoor furniture
picnic basket
planters
rugs
steamer chairs
sundial
tool kit
watering can
wheelbarrow
work table

Cleaning Gear
brushes and brooms
buckets
carpet sweeper or
    shampooer
clothes airer
dustpan and brush
floor polisher
iron and ironing table
mops
rubbish bin
spin dryer
vacuum cleaner
washing machine

General
beach umbrella
bicycle
binoculars
bookcase
book ends
books
briefcase
camera
cassette player
coffee table
curtains
cushions
door chimes
dishwasher
electronic timer
fan
figurine
fireside accessories
games
leather desk set
luggage
magazine rack
medicine chest
mirror
nest of tables
radio
rattan chair
sewing machine
stationery
stereo
typewriter
TV
video
vases
welcome mat
writing desk

WEDDING ANNIVERSARIES

Until the big celebrations after twenty or twenty-five years of marriage, wedding anniversaries tend to be personal rather than public occasions. Many people treat anniversaries much like birthdays. Others choose gifts that can be enjoyed by both partners.

The formal listing of wedding anniversaries is given below. Lists for the first twenty years show many variations. But after that every list agrees.

CLASSICS

Traditional

1 paper (stationery, prints, notebooks, books, magazines)
2 cotton (quilt, cushion, fabrics, pillow covers)
3 leather (luggage, gloves, purse, belt, briefcase, frames)
4 silk or books (scarves, hankies, embroidery, shirt)
5 wood or clocks (breadboard, bowls, decoy duck)
6 iron (gardening equipment, fireside tools)
7 copper, bronze, brass (decorative planters, lamps, cooking equipment)
8 electrical appliances
9 pottery
10 tin or aluminium (kitchen or outdoor equipment)
11 steel
12 silk or linen (tableware, clothing)
13 lace (table accessories)
14 ivory (jewellery, boxes, figures)
15 crystal (glasses, bowls, paperweight, vase, necklace)
20 china (dinnerware, platters, figurine)
25 silver (picture frame, candlesticks, ornaments, jewellery, coins)
30 pearl
35 coral jade
40 ruby
45 sapphire
50 gold (pen and pencil set, picture frame, sampler)
55 emerald
60 diamond

Modern

1 clocks
2 china
3 crystal/glass
4 appliances
5 silver

10 diamond jewellery
12 pearls
15 watches
20 platinum
25 silver
30 diamond

For a traditional gift, choose something from the list above. If lace, steel or copper seem too limiting as gift themes, simply buy a token item made of this, and attach it to a more desirable gift!

Alternatively, check all the classic lists in the book and consider buying two of an item. Finally, if you are really stuck, buy something made of silver — a tray, cutlery, or coffee spoons. You can add to their silver collection year after year.

THE PERSONAL TOUCH

* One red rose — For a superb touch, give one red rose for each year you have been married. This is simple at the beginning and gloriously generous as the years go on. Choose a less expensive gift, like a single chocolate, if that's more manageable.

* Organise a wine or port bottling for the occasion and have special labels printed.

* Give a voucher for a photographic studio portrait to commemorate the occasion.

* For a romantic gift, give a weekend away voucher, a theatre and restaurant voucher or a luxury voucher for a beauty treatment (hair, manicure, sauna and massage).

Note: Check the list on page 81 for more ideas.

BIRTHS AND CHRISTENINGS

Gift giving has always been an important part of christenings. As far back as the Middle Ages, wealthy godparents gave twelve silver spoons as a christening gift, which led to the expression 'born with a silver spoon in his mouth'. For non-churchgoers who may wish to create some tradition of their own, consider holding a backgarden naming ceremony, with friends and relations present. A decorative cake, champagne and a handful of speeches will create the very special and supportive atmosphere of family and friends.

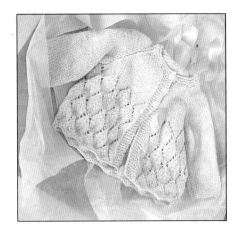

CLASSICS

Give a classic that can develop into a collection: Matchbox car, Beatrix Potter Book, Bunnikins, or the collected works of a great author.

✸ A silver picture frame, hairbrush, cup or napkin ring; a christening gown, quality china baby mugs or porringers.

✸ A single pearl or silver charm. Give one per year up to twenty-one.

out the children. Perhaps the luxury of a morning's shopping, a haircut, a new dress or clothes might be welcomed with open arms.

✸ P.S. More Ideas — camera (Polaroid) and film; photo album; engraved article e.g. spoon; training cups; savings account; room furnishings; nursery pictures; cutlery set; set of name labels; doll's house; mobile; picture books; music box.

THE PERSONAL TOUCH

Although there are excellent baby parcels widely available in shops, your personal creation will be less expensive and more original. As long as you provide plenty of items like zinc and castor oil cream, nappy change lotion, pins, pilchers, powders, shampoos and oil, the parcel will be useful. Wrap your collection in a nappy, a nappy bucket, or a play mat. If you are really stuck, look at the toddler birthday packages too.

✸ If you are good at knitting, sewing, patchwork and needlework there are lots of gift possibilities, e.g. booties; bib; playsuit; jump suit; hat; soft toy; wall hanging; quilt. (See Chapter 5.)

✸ Buy a set of mint coins for the year of birth. You can keep adding to the collection if you wish.

✸ Buy a couple of bottles of vintage (not tawny) port or a case of wine for when the child turns twenty-one.

✸ Promises! Promises! — What does every new parent need? A babysitter, a cooked dinner, a weekend away with-

HOUSEWARMINGS

Moving house is a major event in our lives, often celebrated by throwing a housewarming party. It's fun to acknowledge a new start with a gift as a way of saying good luck for the future.

CLASSICS

A classic gift for this kind of occasion is usually something for the house (e.g. brass house number; letter box; a pair of topiary pines; a dinner gong); a personal gift for the owners (e.g. flowers or chocolates) to help them over the moving hump, or a celebratory gift like a bottle or two of good champagne.

THE PERSONAL TOUCH

✹ Emergency food hamper made up of savoury nibbles, sweets and a bottle of wine to wash it all down with.

✹ Photo album to document the 'before' and 'after' stages — especially if they plan to do renovations or redecorate.

✹ Outdoor Furniture — For the garden or balcony; if they are keen to landscape the new garden include some plants and seeds.

✹ A home-delivered dinner or lunch on moving day, and a morning's help to shift furniture.

✹ Gluwein — Make a big container of gluwein for the housewarming.
Recipe: You'll need lemon slices, 2 cinnamon sticks, ½ teaspoon whole cloves, 4 strips orange peel, ½ cup sugar, 1 cup mixed raisins and whole almonds, 1 bottle dry, red wine. Place all ingredients in bowl and steep for six hours. When ready, simply strain and warm up liquid to serve. As the Swedes say: 'A warm house with warm inhabitants!'

✹ P.S. More Ideas — potpourri; picture hook or frames; rug; lamp; table linen; drawer liners; teatowels; chamois; feather duster; brush and pan; rubbish or compost bin; visitor's book; book ends.
Note: Check the other gift ideas throughout the book, especially the Lifestyle and Special Interest gift ideas on pages 92 and 93.

RETIREMENT

Those wonderful old customs of giving a golden handshake or a gold watch seem to be disappearing as we become increasingly mobile in jobs and lifestyle. People are retiring earlier, with plenty of living ahead, and the gifts we give need to reflect this change of emphasis.

CLASSICS

If the setting and dress is formal, then the gifts need to be formal too — classic, lasting gifts that reflect the occasion and the person's achievements in life.

An original painting, classic accessories, Persian rugs, time pieces, book or record collections, framed prints, silver, gold and china are all appropriate. Try for a gift which is a 'one-off' special item as most people of retirement age have many of the classics already.

THE PERSONAL TOUCH

Retirement can be a sensitive issue but for many people it is the beginning of an exciting new chapter in their lives. It's important to find out about the person's plans and aspirations for the future and present them with an appropriate gift. It may be a collection of essential travel items for their round the world trip; or a parcel of beautiful fabrics and threads for a master patchwork quilter.

Whatever the person's outlook and set of interests, they will need your continued encouragement and support now that they suddenly have more time on their hands. *Your* time with them may well be the best gift of all!

✷ A magazine or newspaper subscription; a National Trust membership; a voucher for a portrait; a hot air balloon ride; a short helicopter flight or a voucher for a job they'd like done.

✷ P.S. More Ideas — bird feeder; book tape; bowling hat; budgie; camera; crossword book; gold fish or other pet; home-made food hamper; large print books; metal detector; page magnifier; personal fan; house plant; season's tickets and chauffeur; shoe rack; silk flowers; stationery; theatre tickets; travel rug; wool and pattern; woollen underblanket; year plates; giant jigsaw; gardener's diary.

Note: Check the gift suggestions through the book for more ideas.

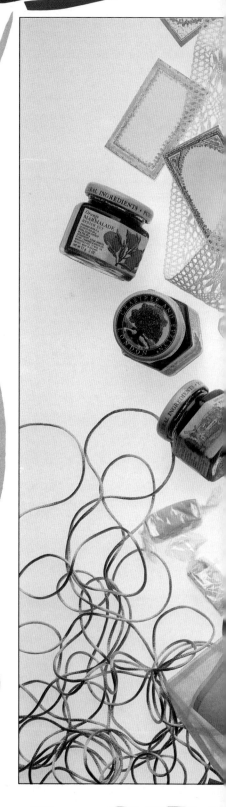

With all the excitement and ritual of gift presentation, it's all too easy to forget that it really is the *thought* that counts.

In this chapter, we've dealt with thorny issues that can take the pleasure out of giving and receiving, such as fears that we've given either too much or too little or worries about trimming a gift list that is straining our budget.

Although there is a certain etiquette to observe on the gifts front, the only unshakeable rule is that you should show your gratitude for both presents and efforts made on your behalf.

8 THE THOUGHT THAT COUNTS

Small tokens of appreciation like chocolates or a posy of flowers are an effective way of saying thank-you to a hostess who has toiled over a dinner party, or showing appreciation to a friend or colleague who has done you a kindness.

Conversely, you can bring cheer to someone in low spirits, such as a hospital patient, with a thoughtful gesture designed to brighten their day — a bowl of potpourri to counteract the antiseptic smell, a jolly poster to liven up the room or even a goldfish or two for company!

The thought often counts most poignantly when you're sending or receiving gifts over great distances — a parcel through the post may be the only tangible contact we have with far-flung friends and family, so we have come up with a wide range of goodies designed to make up an imaginative and thoughtful postal gift.

Whatever your headache about the rules and practicalities of gift-giving, this chapter should provide you with the solution!

Mid City Granny May's Paper Shop   Lois With Love   David Jones   Mid City House and Garden

GIFT ETIQUETTE

TIPS FOR HANDLING PROBLEMS

The most important rule of etiquette for gift-giving is to thank people properly, at the moment the gift is given and after important occasions, with a handwritten note or at the very least, a phonecall.

There are a number of other touchy areas in gift giving that sometimes create concern. Here are some ideas for handling them.

✸ Gifts You Don't Like — If the giver visits regularly, and you care about their feelings, you really need to keep the gift within eyesight. For casual gifts you don't like, simply recycle them while they're new. Someone else will love the vase you loathe.

✸ Stopping Gifts — If your Christmas gift list is getting out of hand, phone friends and say tactfully that you'd like to send a card only this year, or exchange very small home-made gifts.

✸ Unequal Gifts — If someone spends $50 on your gift for Christmas, you are not obliged to reciprocate in kind. The amount you spend on a gift is entirely your decision. The secret is to buy what your budget can comfortably afford. We all know that it's not the cost of a gift that matters but the thought.

✸ Difficult People — Some people just don't enjoy gifts or gift giving. Don't spend hours worrying about what to give them. A simple home-made food item is best, like jam, shortbread or fudge. (Use your time and creative energy thinking up wonderful gifts for those who adore gift giving, because they will really appreciate your efforts.)

✸ People Who Have It All — Lucky people! Buy them an original from a gallery or handicrafts shop; make them a basket of home-made goodies; if you have art and design skills give them one of your own art works e.g. print, painting, ceramic, pottery, fabric work; treat them to a unique experience e.g. hot air balloon ride, or to a night at the opera or theatre.

✸ Big Family Christmas — When the number of relatives you're buying for becomes ridiculous, why not suggest that you have a Christmas Day Lucky Dip, where everyone buys a gift costing $2–$5 maximum? Wrap each gift and place in a bag for the Lucky Dip. This is lots of fun and can take the pressure off big family gift giving occasions. You will be amazed at the variety of gifts you can buy for under $5!

✸ Family Gifts — Instead of agonising over separate gifts for each member of a family buy a family gift. Make up a hamper of food or a box of games; give a set of fabric paints, and some white T-shirts; a big book the whole family can read (an illustrated encyclopaedia); pool or outdoor equipment.

A LITTLE SOMETHING

THANK YOU GIFTS

The best thank you gifts are thoughtful tokens, not full-scale presentations. If you decide to give one of the traditional hostess gifts — flowers, chocolates, wine or home-made goodies, add some panache with your wrapping and presentation.

✸ Flowers — The last thing a busy hostess needs to do when you arrive is to arrange your flowers. Either bring flowers that are ready trimmed and arranged ready to pop into a vase (perhaps that could be part of your gift), or give a posy which needs no work.

A gift of a single rose, or a pot plant is the simplest gift of all.
Note: See Chapter 3 for more ideas.

✸ Chocolates — Even ordinary boxed chocolates look exciting peeping out from a brandy balloon, bunched in a dainty cloth napkin, or nestling in a cane basket. Always unwrap pre-packed truffles or chocolates and rewrap creatively.

PRESENTATION HINTS

☐ Use clear cellophane or silver paper with lots of ribbon and flower trim.
☐ Wrap and place in a tiny gift box.
☐ Re-wrap loose chocolates in cellophane, tying each like a bonbon. This trick makes small numbers of expensive chocolates look superb.
☐ Staple your wrapped peppermint creams inside a special card.

✸ Wine — If you like giving wine as a gift, try to buy something a little unusual. Your hosts may have already chosen the wine for dinner. Choose a bottle of dessert wine, a tokay or port which can be kept for later. Wrap it beautifully, and present it as a gift you've thought about carefully, not something you grabbed at a bottle shop minutes earlier!

✸ Home-Made Goodies — Your orange pomander, or home-made cumquat marmalade in a jar with a fabric print top, matching ribbon tie and informative label will make a special gift. Add the recipe on a card tied at the neck. (See Chapter 4 for more ideas.)

✸ P.S. More Ideas — If your hostess is interested in cooking buy something unusual for her *batterie de cuisine* — a strawberry huller, lemon squeezer, a tiny balloon whisk. Otherwise buy simple gifts like personal toiletries, writing paper or note cards.

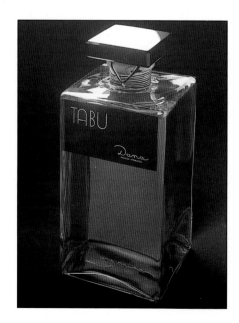

GET WELL SOON

GIFTS FOR INVALIDS

Hospitals can be cold impersonal places so when you are planning a gift, try to think of something that might improve the look of the room; increase the person's comfort or simply give pleasure (books, food, music, hobbies, vouchers).

TO BRIGHTEN UP A HOSPITAL OR BEDROOM

✳ Buy a flowering plant in a colourful pot (part of the gift).
✳ Wrap up a bunch of pretty flowers fresh from your garden (see Chapter 3).
✳ Choose a small fish bowl and a fish or two for company.
✳ A sand picture is interesting to watch.
✳ Have a colourful poster laminated and attach to the wall with blue tac, ready to take down later.
✳ Make a cushion or throw-over for the visitor's chair.

TO MAKE THE PATIENT OR OLDER PERSON MORE COMFORTABLE

✳ a woollen underblanket, bed jacket or bed socks
✳ a triangular pillow with personalised pillow-case, or a back rest
✳ breakfast tray, napkin, ring, and china to match
✳ book light and large print books
✳ cassette recorder, radio, or portable TV, an updated supply of cassettes, plus music and book cassettes
✳ tape your voice reading a book, giving a chapter each visit, or tape your children's voices

FOR PLEASURE

✳ books, comics, magazine subscriptions, crossword books
✳ writing paper, stamps and envelopes
✳ home-made goodies (see Chapter 4)
✳ cheese board, cheeses and biscuits
✳ bird feeder
✳ family photograph collection
✳ a voucher for a visit to the theatre, a concert, or the opera (include a driver and wheelchair arrangements if necessary)
✳ a voucher offering chiropody, a hair set, or a visit to the local botanical gardens for afternoon tea

SEND IT BY MAIL —

GIFTS TO POST

Nothing is more difficult than thinking up new and different gifts to post each year for Christmas and birthdays both locally and overseas. If it becomes impossibly difficult, pluck up the courage to suggest a halt on sending gifts. The other party may be just as relieved as you!

✳ Australiana — For friends overseas, try some of these local goodies as a surprise, an education, or a reminder of how life really is back home.

☐ food parcel — Vegemite (sachets only), instant pavlova, small cherry ripes and violet crumbles

☐ pair of thongs, towelling hat, stockman's hat

☐ prints and posters (scrolled in a cardboard tube)

☐ laminated Australian gift paper for children to use as posters

☐ a wall hanging with Aboriginal design motifs and colours

✳ P.S. More Ideas — book marks; boomerangs; brooches; badges; silver koala charm; handkerchiefs; calendars; airmail paper; hugging koalas; flags; Australian perfume; potpourri; napkins; woven badges; stick pins; cork hat; key ring; spoons; belt; mobile; necklace; colourful posters (for example, by Ken Done); classic Australian books or a contemporary Australian novel.

Note: Post early seamail!

OTHER IDEAS FOR GIFTS TO POST

Buy clothes for children *only* if you are certain about size. Try some of the following suggestions for more original items.

✳ Cassette tape letter featuring you, family and friends.

✳ Vouchers — a magazine subscription, book or record voucher, a voucher for a ten minute overseas phone call.

✳ P.S. More Ideas — unusual belts; jewellery; sets of coins or stamps; blow-up photo of family; picture frames; money; scarves and gloves; sporting

accessories (hats, sweat bands, sox); scrap books; Swiss knife or pocket knife; doilies; napkins; place mats; makeup; bow tie; funny watch; moccasins; cushion cover; piece of fabric; old-fashioned paper fan; tie; wallet; purse; ruler; rubber; playing cards; mobile.

✳ Wraps — Bows simply don't travel well! Instead, use the lattice wrap (see p. 17) and decorate with a flat sticker.

Note: Use post packs where possible. They'll help your gift look great till it arrives safely.

LIFESTYLE AND SPECIAL INTEREST GIFT IDEAS

One of the best ways of coming up with more unusual gift ideas is to look closely at the person's lifestyle and special interests.

The ideas listed here are great starting points and can be presented in many different ways to create just the degree of impact you want. All of these items would make excellent gifts on their own, or can be teamed up with others for a more creative package.

GIFT IDEAS

Book Lovers
book club membership
book ends
book light
book plates (personalised)
book voucher
book stand
desk lamp

Business People
alarm clock
tea maker
colour analysis or image consultation
course in public speaking
lunch box and flask
shoe rack
stress management course

Car Lovers
car manual
car wash brush
car washing kit
car vacuum
de-icer
driving hats
eye-level brake lights
empty petrol can
fire extinguisher
grease gun
jumper leads
mats
magnetic key case
mudflaps
racing gloves
radio
replica Mercedes or Porsche
rags
seat or cushion covers
spark plugs
steering wheel cover or lock
sun blinds
torch
tow rope
tyre pump

Chocoholics
Chocolate lover's package with an assortment of every conceivable type of chocolate, beautifully presented in a clear cellophane shirt box, with a copy of Sandra Boynton's book or calendar. Add a chocolate cook book, or chocolate making kit.
Note: Also see Chapter 4.

Cooks
asparagus steamer
balloon whisk
brioche mould
candy moulds
cappuccino maker
copper bowls
flavoured vinegars
ginger and nutmeg grater
icecream maker
Japanese cooking utensils
kitchen shears
meat thermometer
oyster opener
pestle and mortar
pineapple huller
strawberry huller
wok and utensils
yoghurt maker
Note: Wrap smaller items in a kitchen glove, tea towel, or tablecloth. Also see Chapter 4.

Electronic Whizzes
blank video cassettes
compact discs (CDs)
cordless phone
magazine subscription
Dick Smith Voucher

Epicureans
bunch of wooden utensils
decanters
good cutting knives
kitchen gadgets
ladle
pasta maker
quality bottle of champagne (Dom Perignon)
silver candlesticks
silver wine labels
tablecloths
virgin olive oil
wine cooler

Gardeners
bird bath
bird feeder
garden books
cane baskets
compost maker or bin
flares
flowering plants
fountains
gardening smock
garden vacuum
gargoyles
gazebo
gloves
gnome
hanging basket
herb prints
indoor plants
labels for herbs and spices
lawn trimmer
planters
root rack
seed boxes
seed catalogues
subscription for magazines
sundial
sun hat
terrarium
terracotta pots
thatched bird house
topiary tree or rose
wall planter
watering can or watering systems
weathervane
whipper snipper
wind chimes for the garden
Yates garden guide
Zero weed spray
Note: Also see Chapter 3.

Home Handyperson
assorted tools
axe
battery charger
chainsaw
drill
hacksaw
gumboots
leather apron
paint roller kit
sanders
scrapers
screwdriver set
soldering kit
squeegie
step ladder
storage shed
tool box
waterproof trousers
wood files
worktable

Handicraft Person
handicrafts magazine subscription
new needles (for knitting, sewing or embroidery)
voucher for materials
sampler
tapestry
buttons

ribbons
sequins
doll making kit (with porcelain face, felt, eyes, fabric and glue)

Home Renovators
books on interior design
removators' diary
House and Garden magazine subscription
painting kit (overalls, paint brushes, roller, painting sheets)
picture hooks
putty knife
voucher for materials

New Parents Kit
baby bouncer
baby soap
classic picture story books
cotton wool
face cloths
fitted cot sheets
jump suits
mobiles
name tapes
nappies
nappy pins
Nursing Mother's Association membership
safety harness
shampoo
swabs
towels with hoods
toy basket
Vaseline
wipes
babysitting voucher
bottle of Gripe Water
car seat
dummy

Outdoor Types
air bed
beach umbrella
bird house
bug zapper
camp stool
coolers
picnic hamper
plastic champagne flutes
pool equipment
steamer chairs
Swiss knife
thermos
travel rug
tray and glasses
wine cask cooler

Second-Time-Round Marriages
Often difficult because both partners have received most of the traditional gifts already. Try to choose something they can enjoy in their new life together — a rose bush, a photo album, linen with their names on it, or any other item you can personalise, like a pair of director's chairs. Finally, look at Valentines day again for a romantic gift selection (Chapter 2).

Sports Lovers
bag
balls
bandages
sport books
dencorub
glucose tablets
sun hats
head bands
shoes
sports magazines
mouthguard
odour eaters
sports poster
socks
T-shirt
sweat bands
towels

Holidaymakers
Any one of these gifts is useful for a traveller, holidaymaker, or business person as individual gifts, or made up as a gift package.

envelopes
Alka Seltzer
combination lock
drying line
exchange rate calculator
film
inflatable coathanger
leg wallet
letter writing kit
money belt
notebook
pegs
sewing kit
shoe polishing kit
soap
stingo
suit bag
torch
umbrella
universal adaptor
water boiler
year's subscription to National Geographic

And for any mother or father travelling with children, a bag of tricks containing any of the following: a map (follow the route), cards, paper and coloured pencils, small toys, kaleidoscope, packet of Band-Aids.

The Upmarket Man or Woman
The key is elegance and style. Here are some inspiring ideas for buying gifts for stylish people

antique (lamp, silver spoons, cigarette case or letter opener)
art nouveau object
an antique collector's guide
Beluga caviar
BMW key ring
briefcase
camisole
claret jug
collector's plates
crystal or leather desk set
cumquat tree
gilded china birds
gold key ring
Havana cigars
hip flask
hunting hat
icecream churn
jewellery
Kosta Boda vase
linen and lace handkerchief
mahogany box
pearl or gold necklace
Poison perfume
porcelain figurine
rose bowl
silk pyjamas
shaving brush
smoked salmon
silk tie or shirt
silver amulet
silver buckle
slinky stockings
strawberry and cream set
umbrella
walking stick
watch

Wine or Cocktail Buff
armagnac
books on wine and cocktails
butler's friend
champagne pliers
cheese
coasters
cognac
decanter
glasses
ice bucket
ice hammer
jiggers
magazine
muscat
parasol
shaker
silver wine label
swizzle sticks
walnuts
wine bottle tags
wine cooler

GOOD READING FOR CHILDREN

FIVE-YEAR-OLDS

The Aardvark Who Wasn't Sure, The Cat Who Wanted to Go Home, The Gorilla Who Wanted to Grow Up, The Hen Who Wouldn't Give Up, The Otter Who Wanted to Know, The Owl Who Was Afraid of the Dark, Penguin's Progress Jill Tomlinson, illus. Joanne Cole (Methuen/Magnet paperback)

Babar the Little Elephant books Jean and Laurent de Brunhoff (Methuen/Methuen paperback)

Bad Boys ed. Eileen Colwell, illus. Hans Helweg and others (Viking Kestrel/Puffin paperback)

Boastful Rabbit Ruth Manning-Sanders, illus. James Hodgson (Methuen/Magnet paperback)

The Faber Book of Nursery Stories ed. Barbara Ireson, illus. Shirley Hughes (Faber/Faber paperback)

The Faber Book of Nursery Verse ed. Barbara Ireson, illus. George Adamson (Faber paperback)

The Fairy Tale Treasury ed. Virginia Haviland, illus. Raymond Briggs (Hamish Hamilton/Puffin)

For Me, Me, Me compiled by Dorothy Butler, illus. Megan Gressor (Hodder & Stoughton)

Ginnie Ted Greenwood (Viking Kestrel/Fontana Lions paperback)

The Golden Treasury of Poetry ed. Louis Untermeyer, illus. Joan Walsh Anglund (Collins)

Hansel and Gretel Susan Jeffers (Hamish Hamilton)

Hedgehog and Puppy Dog Tales Ruth Manning-Sanders, illus. James Hodgson (Methuen/Magnet paperback)

How the Whale Became and Other Stories Ted Hughes, illus. George Adamson (Puffin paperback)

Johnny Oswaldtwistle Kathleen Hersom, illus. Lesley Smith (Methuen)

Little Tim and the Brave Sea Captain Edward Ardizzone (Viking Kestrel/Puffin)

The Little Yellow Taxi and his Friends Ruth Ainsworth, illus. Gary Inwood (Lutterworth)

Lotta's Bike, Lotta's Christmas Surprise, Lotta Leaves Home and *The Mischievous Martens* Astrid Lindgren, illus. Ilon Wikland (Methuen paperback)

Possum Magic Julie Vivas (Omnibus Books)

The Macquarie Bedtime Story Book ed. Rosalind Price (Macquarie Library)

Mary Kate and the Jumble Bear Helen Morgan, illus. Shirley Hughes (Puffin paperback)

The Oakapple Wood stories (Eight separate, small volumes) Jenny Partridge (World's Work)

Roger Was a Razor Fish compiled by Jill Bennett, illus. Maureen Roffey (The Bodley Head/Scholastic paperback)

Smiley Tiger Barbara Willard, illus. Laszlo Acs (Julia MacRae)

Stories for Five-Year-Olds and Other Young Readers and *Stories for the Under-Fives* both ed. Stephen and Sara Corrin, illus. Shirley Hughes (Faber/Puffin paperback)

Tales of Joe and Timothy Dorothy Edwards, illus. Reintje Venema (Methuen/Magnet paperback)

There's a Hippopotamus on Our Roof Eating Cake Hazel Edwards (Hodder and Stoughton)

The Ten Tales of Shellover Ruth Ainsworth, illus. Antony Maitland (Deutsch/Puffin paperback)

Tiny Tim ed. Jill Bennett, illus. Helen Oxenbury (Heinemann/Fontana Lions paperback)

To Read and To Tell Norah Montgomerie, illus. Margery Gill (The Bodley Head)

The Useless Donkeys Lydia Pender, illus. Judith Cowell (Methuen)

When a Goose Meets a Moose Chosen by Clare Scott-Mitchell, illlus. Louise Hogan (Bell & Hyman)

Wombat Stew Marcia K. Vaughan (Ashton Scholastic)

Would You Rather John Burningham (Jonathan Cape)

The Young Puffin Book of Verse compiled by Barbara Ireson, illus. Gioia Fiammenghi (Puffin paperback)

SIX-YEAR-OLDS

Alexander and the Terrible, Horrible, No Good, Very Bad Day Judith Viorst (Angus and Robertson)

The Amazing Koalas Peter Campbell (Methuen/Magnet paperback)

Amelia Bedelia Peggy Parish, illus. Fritz Siebel (World's Work)

Animalia Graeme Base (Viking/Kestrel)

Are You My Mother? P. D. Eastman (Collins/Collins paperback)

The Big Stink Sheila Lavelle, illus. Lisa Kopper (Heinemann)

A Box for Benny Leila Berg, illus. Jillian Willett (Hodder & Stoughton/Methuen paperback)

Burglar Bill Janet and Allan Ahlberg (Heinemann)

The Bus under the Leaves Margaret Mahy, illus. Margery Gill (Dent/Puffin paperback)

Captain Pugwash and the Fancy-dress Party, Captain Pugwash and the Mutiny, Captain Pugwash and the Midnight Feast and *Captain Pugwash and the Wreckers* John Ryan (The Bodley Head/Puffin paperback)

Days With Frog and Toad, Frog and Toad All Year, Frog and Toad Are Friends, Frog and Toad Together all by Arnold Lobel (World's Work/Puffin paperback)

Dragon Trouble Penelope Lively, illus. Valerie Littlewood (Heinemann)

Far Out Brussel Sprout June Factor (Oxford University Press)

The Ghost Ship Catherine Sefton, illus. Martin Ursell (Hamish Hamilton)

The Gingerbread Rabbit Randall Jarrell, illus. Garth Williams (Macmillan/Fontana Lions paperback)

Harry's Aunt Sheila Lavelle, illus. Jo Davies (Hamish Hamilton)

Helter Skelter: Stories for six-year-olds Pamela Oldfield (ed.), illus. Linda Birch (Blackie/Knight paperback)

I Will Build You a House compiled by Dorothy Butler, illus. Megan Gressor (Hodder & Stoughton)

Jane's Amazing Woolly Jumper and *Polly's Dance* Judith Hindley, illus. Jill Bennett (Patrick Hardy)

A Lion in the Meadow and Five Other Favourites Margaret Mahy, various illustrators (Dent/Puffin paperback)

Little Bear, Little Bear's Friend, Little Bear's Visit and *Father Bear Comes Home* Elsie Holmelund Minarik, illus. Maurice Sendak (World's Work/Puffin paperback)

Meeko and Mirabel Linda Allen, illus. Linda Birch (Hamish Hamilton)

Mr and Mrs Hay the Horse illus. Colin McNaughton, *Mr Biff the Boxer* illus. Janet Ahlberg and *Mrs Lather's Laundry* Allan Ahlberg, illus. André Amstutz (Viking Kestrel/Puffin paperback)

Mrs Gaddy and the Ghost and *The Crow and Mrs Gaddy* Wilson Gage, illus. Marylin Hafner (The Bodley Head/ Scholastic paperback)

A Necklace of Raindrops Joan Aiken, illus. Jan Pienkowski (Cape/Puffin paperback)

The New Golden Land Anthology ed. Judith Elkin, illus. Vanessa Julian-Ottie and others (Viking Kestrel/ Puffin paperback)

Oh, Abigail! Moira Miller, illus. Doreen Caldwell (Methuen/Magnet paperback)

Once Upon a Rhyme: 101 Poems for Young Children ed. Sara and Stephen Corrin, illus. Jill Bennett (Faber/ Puffin paperback)

The Rainy Picnic and Outing for Three Pamela Rogers, illus. Priscilla Clive (Puffin paperback)

Ramona the Pest Beverly Cleary, illus. Louis Darling (Hamish Hamilton/ Puffin paperback). Other titles: *Beezus and Ramona, Ramona and her Father, Ramona and her Mother, Ramona the Brave* and *Ramona Quimby, Age 8*. Henry Huggins titles: *Henry and Beezus, Henry and the Clubhouse* and *Henry and Ribsy*.

Stories for Six-Year-Olds and Other Young Readers Sara and Stephen Corrin, illus. Shirley Hughes (Faber/ Puffin paperback)

Tales for Telling Leila Berg, illus. Danuta Laskowska (Methuen/ Magnet paperback)

Tales from Grimm Wanda Gag (Faber/ Faber paperback)

Tales of Oliver Pig Jean van Leeuwen, illus. Arnold Lobel (The Bodley Head/Fontana paperback)

Ursula Bear Sheila Lavelle, illus. Thelma Lambert (Hamish Hamilton/Beaver Books paperback)

Winnie-the-Pooh and *The House at Pooh Corner* A. A. Milne, illus. Ernest Shepard (Methuen/Methuen paperback)

SEVEN-YEAR-OLDS

Adventures of the Little Wooden Horse Ursula Moray Williams, illus. Peggy Fortnum (Puffin paperback)

Ardizzone's Hans Andersen Stephen Corrin, illus. Edward Ardizzone (Deutsch)

Beastly Boys and Ghastly Girls ed. William Cole, illus. Tomi Ungerer (Methuen/Methuen paperback)

The Beautiful Culpeppers Marion Upington, illus. Louis Slobodkin (Harrap)

The Birthday Mary Cockett, illus. Doreen Caldwell (Hodder & Stoughton)

Bottersnikes and Gumbles S. A. Wakefield (Collins)

The Brothers Grimm: Popular Folk Tales Brian Alderson, illus. Michael Foreman (Gollancz)

Casey, the Utterly Impossible Horse Anita Feagles, illus. Roger Smith (Gollancz/Puffin paperback)

Cautionary Tales for Children Hilaire Belloc, illus. B. T. B. and Nicolas Bentley (Duckworth)

Dorrie and the Wizard's Spell Patricia Coombs (World's Work/Puffin paperback)

The Dragon of an Ordinary Family Margaret Mahy, illus. Helen Oxenbury (Heinemann)

The Dwarfs of Nosegay Paul Biegel, illus. Babs van Wely (Blackie/Puffin paperback).

Fairy Tales Terry Jones, illus. Michael Foreman (Pavilion/Puffin paperback)

Fantastic Mr Fox Roald Dahl, illus. Jill Bennett (Allen & Unwin/Puffin paperback)

Feelings Aliki (Bodley Head)

Fifty Favourite Fairy Tales ed. Kathleen Lines, illus. Margery Gill (The Bodley Head)

Follow That Bus! Pat Hutchins, illus. Laurence Hutchins (The Bodley Head/Fontana Lions paperback)

Four Dolls Rumer Godden, illus. Pauline Baynes (Macmillan)

Gobbolino, the Witch's Cat Ursula Moray Williams (Harrap/Puffin paperback)

The Ha Ha Bonk Book Janet and Allan Ahlberg (Viking Kestrel/Puffin paperback)

Hans Andersen: His Classic Fairy Tales Erik Haugaard, illus. Michael Foreman (Gollancz/Gollancz paperback)

The Illustrated Treasury of Australian Stories and Verse For Children Barbara Ker Wilson (Nelson)

The Julian Stories Ann Cameron, illus. Ann Strugnell (Gollancz/Fontana Lions paperback)

The Juniper Tree and Other Tales from Grimm ed. Lore Segal, illus. Maurice Sendak (The Bodley Head)

Little Bear's Feather Evelyn Davies, illus. Jane Paton (Hamish Hamilton)

The Magic Finger Roald Dahl, illus. Pat Marriott (Allen & Unwin/Puffin paperback)

Old Peter's Russian Tales Arthur Ransome, illus. Faith Jaques (Cape/ Puffin paperback)

Peter Pan and Wendy May Byron, illus. Mabel Lucie Attwell (Hodder & Stoughton)

Puppy Summer Meindert Dejong, illus. Anita Lobel (Lutterworth)

The Rainbow Serpent Dick Roughsey (Collins)

Revolting Rhymes Roald Dahl (Puffin)

Rooms to Let Margaret Mahy, illus. Jenny Williams (Dent)

Stories for Seven-Year-Olds and *More Stories for Seven-Year-Olds* Sara and Stephen Corrin, illus. Shirley Hughes (Faber/Puffin paperback)

Thing Robin Klein, illus. Alison Lester (Oxford)

The Three Toymakers, Malkin's Mountain and *The Toymaker's Daughter* Ursula Moray Williams, illus. Shirley Hughes (Hamish Hamilton)

A Time to Laugh: Funny Stories for Children ed. Sara and Stephen Corrin, illus. Gerald Rose (Faber paperback)

The Village Dinosaur Phyllis Arkle, illus. Eccles Williams (Brockhampton Press/Puffin paperback)

Wildcat Wendy and the Peekaboo Kid Nancy Chambers, illus. James Hodgson (Hamish Hamilton/ Fontana Lions paperback)

You Can't Catch Me! Michael Rosen, illus. Quentin Blake (Deutsch/Puffin paperback)

EIGHT-YEAR-OLDS PLUS

All Sorts of Poems ed. Ann Thwaite (Methuen paperback)

Angry River Ruskin Bond, illus. Trevor Stubley (Hamish Hamilton)

Arabel and Mortimer, Mortimer's Cross, Mortimer Says Nothing and Tales of Arabel's Raven Joan Aiken, illus. Quentin Blake (Cape)

Beaver Towers Nigel Hinton, illus. Peter Rush (Abelard-Schuman/Knight paperback)

Bellabelinda and the No-Good Angel Ursula Moray Williams, illus. Glenys Ambrus (Chatto & Windus)

The Best Christmas Pageant Ever Barbara Robinson, illus. Judith Gwyn Brown (Faber) pub. in paperback under the title The Worst Kids in the World (Beaver Books)

The BFG Roald Dahl, illus. Quentin Blake (Cape/Puffin paperback)

Brother Dusty-Feet Rosemary Sutcliff, illus. C. Walter Hodges (Oxford)

Charlie and the Chocolate Factory Roald Dahl, illus. Faith Jaques (Allen & Unwin/Puffin paperback)

Charlotte's Webb E. B. White, illus. Garth Williams (Hamish Hamilton/Puffin paperback)

Chips and Jessie Shirley Hughes (The Bodley Head/Fontana Lions paperback)

Christabel Alison Morgan, illus. Mariella Jennings (Julia MacRae)

C.L.U.T.Z. Marilyn Wilkes, illus. Larry Ross (Gollancz/Piccolo paperback)

Conrad, the Factory Made Boy Christine Nostlinger (Beaver paperback)

Dinner at Alberta's Russell Hoban, illus. James Marshall (Cape/Puffin paperback)

Eight Children and a Truck and Eight Children Move House Anne-Cath Vestly, illus. John Dyke (Methuen)

Fairy Tales Alison Uttley, chosen by Kathleen Lines, illus. Ann Strugnell (Puffin paperback)

Fantastic Mr Fox Roald Dahl, illus. Jill Bennett (Allen & Unwin/Puffin paperback)

Farmer Boy Laura Ingalls Wilder, illus. Garth Williams (Lutterworth/Puffin paperback)

The First Fleet Alan Boardman (Five Mile Press)

The Ghost and Bertie Boggin Catherine Sefton, illus. Jill Bennett (Faber/Puffin paperback)

Grimble and Grimble at Christmas Clement Freud, illus. Quentin Blake (Puffin paperback)

Grump and the Hairy Mammoth Derek Sampson, illus. Simon Stern (Methuen/Methuen paperback)

The Hobbit J. R. R. Tolkien (Allen & Unwin/Allen & Unwin paperback)

The Hundred and One Dalmatians Dodie Smith (Heinemann/Piccolo paperback)

The Jolly Postman Janet and Allan Ahlberg (Heinemann)

I Like This Poem ed. Kaye Webb, illus. Antony Maitland (Viking Kestrel/Puffin paperback)

The Iron Man Ted Hughes, illus. Andrew Davidson (Faber/Faber paperback)

It's Funny When You Look at It Colin West (Century Hutchinson)

It's Too Frightening for Me Shirley Hughes (Hodder & Stoughton/Puffin paperback)

James and the Giant Peach Roald Dahl, illus. Nancy Ekholm Burkert (Allen & Unwin/Puffin paperback)

Janni's Stork Rosemary Harris, illus. Juan Wijngaard (Blackie)

The Jungle Book Rudyard Kipling (Macmillan/Macmillan paperback)

Just So Stories Rudyard Kipling (Macmillan, Quarto Edition/Macmillan paperback)

King Arthur and his Knights Anthony Mockler, illus. Nick Harris (Oxford)

The Load of Unicorn Cynthia Harnett (Methuen)

The Lord of the Rings J. R. R. Tolkien (Allen & Unwin/Allen & Unwin paperback)

The Magic Doll and Other Stories ed. Naomi Lewis, illus. Harold Jones (Methuen paperback)

The Magic Finger Roald Dahl, illus. Pat Marriott (Allen & Unwin/Puffin paperback)

One Thousand and One Arabian Nights Geraldine McCaughrean, illus. Stephen Lavis (Oxford University Press)

The Peopling of Australia Percy Tresize (Collins)

The Perfect Hamburger Alexander McCall Smith, illus. Laszlo Acs (Hamish Hamilton/Puffin paperback)

The Phantom Fisherboy Ruth Ainsworth, illus. Shirley Hughes (Deutsch)

Pippi Goes Aboard, Pippi in the South Seas and Pippi Longstocking Astrid Lindgren, illus. Richard Kennedy (Oxford/Puffin paperback)

Please, Mrs Butler Allan Ahlberg, illus. Fritz Wegner (Viking Kestrel/Puffin paperback)

Poems for Nine-year-olds and under ed. Kit Wright, illus. Michael Foreman (Viking Kestrel/Puffin paperback)

The Queen Elizabeth Story Rosemary Sutcliff, illus. C. Walter Hodges (Oxford)